CRAWL SPACE SCIENCE
What to Have Done... *and Why*

Lawrence Janesky

Crawl Space Science
What to Have Done and Why

by Lawrence Janesky
edited by Dan Fitzgerald and Richard Fencil

Published by:
Basement Systems, Inc.
60 Silvermine Road, Seymour, CT 06483
800-640-1500
203-881-5090

ISBN: 0-9776457-2-X

Visit us at www.basementsystems.com

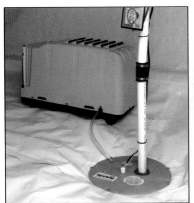

"Even at this early date, we calculate that we have saved our customers worldwide 3.2 million dollars in natural gas, electricity and heating oil <u>each year</u> – forever, and ultimately many times more in rot repairs and mold remediation."

– Lawrence Janesky
January 2006

This book is dedicated to the hard-working Basement Systems dealers and CleanSpace Installers worldwide, who solve the mystery of how to create healthier, more energy efficient environments for homeowners with crawl spaces everyday.

Table of Contents

Forward

> **This is not a do-it-yourself book because crawl space repair is not a do-it-yourself job. It's hard work, and takes too much specialized knowledge, skill, and equipment.**
>
> **The purpose of this book is to give you enough knowledge to make an educated decision on how to know what work needs to be done to your home, who to do it, and why.**

A family in Tennessee has 37 floor joists replaced in their eight-year old home.

- A South Carolina mother takes her four-year-old daughter to the doctor, again, desperately searching for a medical solution to the child's serious asthma and allergy-like symptoms.
- A Connecticut condominium board meets and again the main topic of the discussion is additional rot repairs needed. They approve yet another major expense – this time for $172,000 for the 36 units.
- An Indiana homeowner tries to lower his home energy costs, making frequent trips to the local hardware store for caulk, weather-stripping, and insulation for his attic, all with little results to his household fuel bills.
- An Oregon attorney writes a lawsuit for his clients mold claim, trying to include all the target plaintiffs.
- An Arkansas homeowner goes to work after making arrangements for someone to let the exterminator into the house to deal with the unwanted pest problem that he can never seem to get rid of.
- A Virginia family hires a firm to perform expensive mold remediation in their home and considers moving out until the work can be completed.

Why? Why is all this happening? Answer – Dirt crawl spaces. There is no more serious and common defect with housing than vented dirt crawl spaces.

There is no shred of evidence or science that says vented dirt crawl spaces make sense – and tons of evidence, right before our eyes, that says they are a serious problem. Yet over 250,000 new homes and thousands of additions are built each year with dirt crawl spaces. There are now 26 million of them. The building code not only allows dirt crawl spaces, but actually made the problem much worse by requiring them to be vented. Homeowners, and the U.S. economy are paying the price in so many ways. It's time for something to be done – right now.

Watch out for old fashioned ideas still offered that don't work.

CAUTION

Your home costs money to operate – to heat and cool, and to maintain. A vented dirt crawl space raises your heating and cooling cost 15% (to 25%) every month, and makes it very likely you'll have a big expense for mold removal and/or rotted wood replacement (guaranteed in the Southeast US).

And if it's worth owning a home with a dirt crawl space at all, it is certainly worth fixing...

Your local authorized CleanSpace Installer may have given you this book. Otherwise find your local CleanSpace Installer by calling Basement Systems *international headquarters* at **1-800-640-1500** or visit www.basementsystems.com.

Crawl Space & Basement Specialists™

What Do You Want?

Take the Quiz –

Important

Finish the next two thoughts by choosing A, B, or C.

I want –

❏ A) Mold or Rot
> You probably already have this, you can stop reading now.

❏ B) Just a little mold and rot
> Then treat your crawl space with the wrong methods.

☑ C) NO mold or rot in my house
> Then get it right the first time.

I want my monthly heating and cooling bills to be –

❏ A) As high as possible without me realizing there is a problem.
> You probably already have this, you can stop reading now.

❏ B) A little lower, but I am still willing to pay more.
> Then fix your crawl space half way.

☑ C) As low as reasonably possible!
> Then have it fixed right. Don't cheap out.

So the premise of this book is that you want a mold and rot free crawl space and energy bills as low as possible! Read on...

How to Use this Book
A Reader's Guide

There are 11 brief chapters, each dealing with a specific aspect of achieving your clean, crawl space goal (See the Table of Contents). There are photographs and sidebars in each chapter to help communicate a point. In addition there are seven different symbols which have different meanings—

Important

This is important!

You'll Love This!

You will love the results from this!

CAUTION

Beware, don't make this mistake.

This is a BIG IDEA!

This subject is very important in getting the results you want.

Side Note

Additional Information

Important to Save Energy

This is important to save on heating and cooling costs.

Trade Secrets

Insider Information

This is industry insider information.

Crawl Space Terms of the Trade

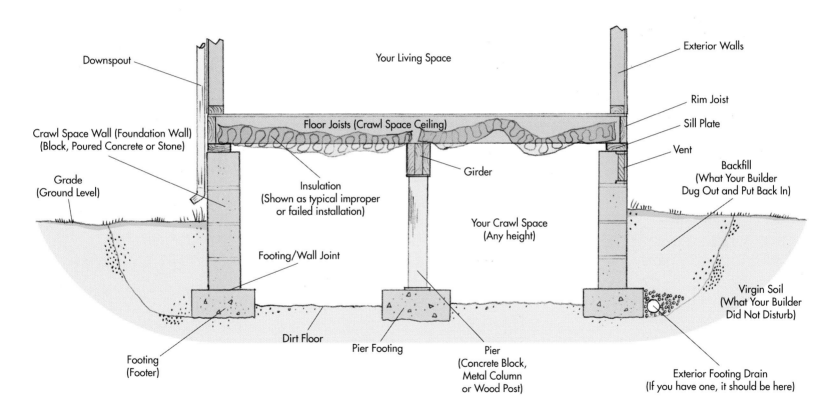

Downspout

Your Living Space

Exterior Walls

Crawl Space Wall (Foundation Wall) (Block, Poured Concrete or Stone)

Rim Joist

Sill Plate

Floor Joists (Crawl Space Ceiling)

Vent

Grade (Ground Level)

Girder

Backfill (What Your Builder Dug Out and Put Back In)

Insulation (Shown as typical improper or failed installation)

Your Crawl Space (Any height)

Footing/Wall Joint

Virgin Soil (What Your Builder Did Not Disturb)

Dirt Floor

Footing (Footer)

Pier Footing

Pier (Concrete Block, Metal Column or Wood Post)

Exterior Footing Drain (If you have one, it should be here)

Chapter 1

The Dirt Crawl Space Problem

The problem is moisture inside of a building – particularly because a building is made from organic materials, filled with objects made from organic materials, and lived in by people.

Outdoor Air

The moisture comes from two sources – the ground and the outdoor air.

Ground

Moisture From The Ground

On paper, in theory and in reality, exposed earth contributes a lot of water vapor into the crawl space air. The earth is damp, and as that damp soil dries into the house, the water vapor moves upward into the house. In most climates where there are dirt crawl spaces, you can never dry the earth, and this invisible stream of water vapor from the exposed earth in a crawl space goes on forever.

Groundwater leakage lays in a crawl space slowly evaporating into the house.

There are several other ways water gets into a house. Groundwater seeps, leaks and even rushes into many crawl spaces. It enters under the footing, between the footing and the walls, right through block walls, and through cracks in poured walls. After it seeps in, it just lays there in puddles, slowly evaporating upward into the house.

Exposed earth adds a continuous stream of water vapor into your home.

Trouble in Paradise

You can't tell from here that the crawl space in this home is costing its owners extra money in heating and cooling costs and is rotting the house from the inside out.

Wood + Water = Bad

Block walls are porous and have lots of imperfect mortar joints in them. They suck up water from the ground, making a wet surface on the inside of the crawl space walls to evaporate into the house.

Damp air from the ground passes right through the block walls. Builders do not plan on these things happening. And that's why they happen.

Crawl spaces often have poor or non-existent exterior footing drains and waterproof exterior wall coatings. In Oregon and other places, builders fit their dirt crawl spaces with a drain inside the crawl space in a low spot – obviously knowing and planning on the crawl spaces leaking, and making a way for the water to flow out. This does not help the water vapor issue one bit.

In fact, water does very little to ruin a home with a dirt crawl space. The water seldom if ever touches any of the parts of a house that get ruined, like floor joists and sill plates. It's the water <u>vapor</u>, also called Relative Humidity, that kills the house. Understanding where high relative humidity comes from and how to control it is what almost everyone has missed.

Block walls allow water and water vapor in easily.

It's 2006. We sent a man to the moon...

38 years ago, but we can't figure out how to keep our houses with dirt crawl spaces from being eaten by mold and fungus. That is what this book is about. It is the biggest "loophole" in the building code. Plumbers, electricians, home inspectors, pest control operators, etc., crawl in these godforsaken, nasty, dirty, drafty, wet, moldy, rotting, places everyday.
It's time we said,
"This isn't right!
This is
bad!"

Water From The Air

Air is a very efficient way to move water. Air, including humid air, moves easily in and out of spaces. It's all around us, and moves in vast quantities through the largest and smallest of spaces. Air brings its moisture content with it wherever it goes.

Here's the "magic", or "black magic" part. When air is heated or cooled, it's relative humidity changes. Warm air holds more moisture than cold air. The relative humidity of air goes down by 2.2% for every degree we heat it and up by 2.2% for every degree we cool it.

This **is a** **BIG** **IDEA!**

! Important

How Summer Venting Makes a Crawl Space Moisture Problem Worse

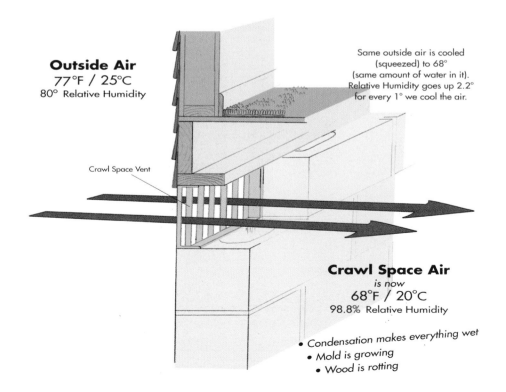

Outside Air
77°F / 25°C
80° Relative Humidity

Same outside air is cooled (squeezed) to 68° (same amount of water in it). Relative Humidity goes up 2.2° for every 1° we cool the air.

Crawl Space Vent

Crawl Space Air
is now
68°F / 20°C
98.8% Relative Humidity

• Condensation makes everything wet
• Mold is growing
• Wood is rotting

Side Note

Ground Temperature

The average temperature of the ground in your area is the same as the average annual outdoor temperature in your area. Whatever that number is, clearly it is less than the temperature of the air that enters your crawl space in the summer.

1 "Water does very little to ruin a home with a dirt crawl space. It's the water vapor that kills the house."

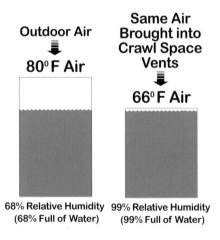

Outdoor Air	Same Air Brought into Crawl Space Vents
80° F Air	66° F Air

68% Relative Humidity (68% Full of Water)   99% Relative Humidity (99% Full of Water)

Got it?

Crawl spaces are cool, because the earth is 55 degrees year round (ground surface temperatures vary based on season and geography). So when we bring warm humid air into a crawl space, the air is cooled, and the relative humidity goes up. High relative humidity causes rot, mold, energy loss, and attracts pests.

So here's the problem. Many years ago when some guys were writing the building code, they rationalized that since we have a lot of moisture from the ground in our dirt crawl spaces, we need to do something about it. They figured that if they vented a crawl space, the moisture would flow out through the vents.

Maybe it was too obvious. Maybe they didn't notice how it rains twice a week or so, and didn't stop to think about what causes it to rain. Maybe it didn't occur to the authors of the building code that when it was a damp day, that they'd be venting the crawl space with damp air. And when it was a cold day, they'd be venting the crawl space with cold air. And when it was a hot day, they'd be venting the crawl space with hot air. And they certainly didn't know about or consider that air flows upward in a house.

On cold days, we are venting our crawl spaces with cold air.

On hot days,
we are venting
our crawl spaces
with hot air.

On wet days, we are venting our
crawl spaces with wet air.

Crawl Space Foundation Types

Concrete Block Walls

❖ Most common and still used today. Hollow and very porous.

Cinder Block Walls

"Cinder Block" is concrete block made with the uncombusted remains of coal fires. The dark gray cinders were readily available and lightweight, but also made the blocks very porous and leaky. Cinder blocks have not been manufactured for 50 years or so.

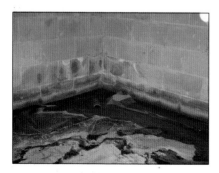

Block walls are the easiest and cheapest material to build a foundation with. They are also the least resistant to water and air going through them since there are so many joints in the wall. To make matters worse, each block has hollow cavities in them and when they are stacked on top of each other they form one big honeycomb of air space in them. Block walls have been referred to as "God's gift to waterproofing contractors."

Trade Secrets

Insider Information

Poured Concrete Walls

❖ Solid concrete. More common in newer homes. Unless there is a hole, crack or pipe penetration, water and air do not go through them.

Stone Walls

❖ Common in older homes. They leak water and air.

Chapter 2

Venting Crawl Spaces

Sometimes the solution is worse
than the problem. And sometimes
the solution is not a solution,
and worse than the problem.

That's what venting a crawl space is.

Venting On A Hot Summer Day

When we say "relative humidity" we mean how full of water the air is relative to the maximum amount of water it can hold at a given temperature.

Crawl space vents – a major problem.

Let's look at what happens on a hot summer day. You have 84-degree air with 75% relative humidity entering your vents. Your crawl space is 66 degrees, but the surface temperature of your walls, dirt floor and floor joists is 62 degrees. What will happen when this air comes in (supposedly to vent the moisture out and makes things better)?

Even the non-technical person can follow this simple discussion on relative humidity and dew points. Understanding this is critical to the vented crawl space problem.

For every one degree we cool the air, the relative humidity goes up by 2.2%, because cool air holds less water than warm air. So looking at our summertime situation, the difference between the outside air we let in at 84 degrees, and the crawl space at 62 degrees, is 22 degrees. 22 degrees multiplied by 2.2% is a 48.4% increase in relative humidity.

Our 84-degree air started out with 75% relative humidity; in other words at 84-degrees it was 75% full of water. We cooled it to 62 degrees so we have to add 48.4% to the relative humidity. So that's 123.4% relative humidity. But wait a minute; we can't have over 100% relative humidity. Why not? Because at 100% the air can not hold any more water and must give up its moisture.

A hygrometer measures relative humidity. These are available for as little as $15.

2 | Vents are good for more than letting hot, wet, or cold air in, they can let in water too.

The ceiling, the insulation, and even the light bulb drip with water as warm humid air gives up it's moisture on cool surfaces.

What do we mean, "give up its moisture?" We mean it will either rain, or it will come out on surfaces as condensation. When the relative humidity reaches 100%, we call this the dewpoint – the point at which the air gives up its moisture.

When this warm humid air enters a crawl space, if the crawl space air was colder than the crawl space surfaces, it would rain in the crawl space. But that is never the case. The source of the cold is the earth, and the source of the warmth is the air coming in from the vents, so the surfaces in your crawl space are always colder than the air in a crawl space.

So on this summer day, we get condensation. Which means our crawl space walls get wet. The dirt surface of the floor gets wet. Our air ducts get wet, especially if we have the air conditioning on because the ducts are cold. Our cold water pipes get wet. These surfaces are the coldest.

Our floor joists, girders, sill plates and insulation get wet with condensation. As the insulation gets wet, it gets heavy and falls down to the crawl space floor.

Having high humidity in a crawl space also causes all porous material to soak up moisture from the air like a sponge. There is a direct correlation between relative humidity and wood moisture content. Wood in a damp environment will become damp itself – and damp wood rots, and mold grows on it.

The moisture content of wood is roughly proportional to the Relative Humidity of the surrounding air.

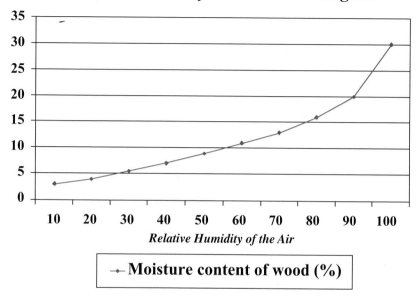

Relative Humidity of the Air

—•— **Moisture content of wood (%)**

This chart shows something that is easy to understand – The wetter the air gets, the wetter the wood gets.

All these wet surfaces in a crawl space will eventually have to dry to somewhere. So let's say we had a few hot summer days which caused condensation in our crawl space. Then the next four or five days are cooler and mild. Is the problem over? No way. After the hot days we are left with a crawl space with wet surfaces everywhere. They dry into the crawl space air over the next weeks and months – and meanwhile mold and wood destroying fungi are having a party, eating your house.

Sound the Alarm

Even the concrete beams and columns in this fire station crawl space are no match for the destructive crawl space environment.

2

The town spent hundreds of thousands of dollars restoring the floor system above the crawl space.

Venting On A Spring or Fall Day

When it's wet out, vents use that wet air "to dry your crawl space."

Of course my examples are for a four-season climate, like much of the U.S. has. However, if you are in the Southern U.S., then you know that my summer example is what you have (and worse) most of the year. If you are in Maine, then you know that my summer examples are for two or three months out of the year, and the winter examples are for longer periods.

If we have a day that is 72 degrees outside, just room temperature, and it is a humid day such as 80%, then when we bring this air into our crawl space to make things better, it will cause condensation. 80% relative humidity (RH) air cooled ten degrees increases its RH by 22%, which is over 100%, which means we have condensation in our crawl space. Is this an extremely hot day? No, it's a normal room-temperature day outside, and we still have a wet crawl space. Let's say it's not so humid. Let's say it's only 60% RH outside. We cool our 72 degree 60% RH air when we bring it into the crawl space to 62 degrees and increase the RH by 22% to 82%. That's less than 100% so we are good right? Wrong! Mold and fungus and rot happen at over 70% RH, and some can thrive at less than that. 82% RH in our crawl space is way more than we want and very unhealthy.

So far, we have learned that venting doesn't work because it doesn't get rid of the dampness (and wetness) in our crawl space, but increases it instead.

So desperate were these homeowners to find a solution, they turned an entire hatchway door into a vent by putting a big screen on it. This only made the problem worse in the summer, and froze their water pipes and caused serious heat loss in the winter.

Venting On A Cool or Winter Day

If the RH of air goes up when we cool it, it goes down when we heat it. So if we vent our crawl spaces in the winter and bring in 35 degree air with 60% RH, and we warm that air in our 62 degree crawl space, the RH goes to 3%. With this dry air we can begin to dry our crawl space. Of course the dry cold air mixes with the crawl space air and cools the crawl space, and we have water evaporating from the earth into the crawl space air, so we never achieve 3% RH in our crawl space, but materials dry out and there is no condensation.

Hey, we're drying our crawl space with vents now! This is great, right? Well, if you like high energy bills, cold floors and cold drafts, then this is for you! (Read on for more information on energy penalties).

When it's cold out, vents let cold air in under our feet. It makes no sense!

2

Chapter 3

Why are Crawl Space Floors Dirt Anyway?
And Why You Should Care!

I have often pondered this question. All areas of the country have a mix of crawl spaces, basements and slab on grade construction. I come from an area where basements are more common than crawl spaces. I have often wondered —"Why do they treat crawl spaces different than basements?" They are not different other than the ceiling height is lower in a crawl space, and yet to this day, they have different codes for basements and crawl spaces.

A dirt crawl space in California gives the homeowners trouble.

The only reason to build a home with a dirt crawl space is to save money. A dirt crawl space is cheaper than a concrete floor. But for that matter, I guess that's why there are lots of building defects. If money were not an obstacle, builders could build the perfect house. But money is an obstacle. So it's pay now or pay later for homeowners. Still, to me, the damage from having a dirt crawl space is so significant, and so expensive, that they should be "out-lawed".

We should never build a home with a dirt crawl space again, even if it costs a few bucks more to do it right. Simply put, a house with a dirt crawl space is dysfunctional, and a dysfunctional house is not worth building – at any price.

If we think about what you would do and not do in a basement, the same rules should apply to a crawl space. In this modern day we would never have a dirt floor basement – so why do we have dirt floor crawl spaces? We would never vent a basement, so why vent a crawl space?

If you went down into a friend's basement in the winter, and saw a window open, or many windows open for that matter, you'd tell your friend to "Close the windows, it's cold down here!" You might even add the word "dummy". Yet we put big holes in our crawl space walls and accept it as normal in the name of making things better. It does not make things better. The Emperor has no clothes!

"A house with a dirt crawl space is dysfunctional, and a dysfunctional house is not worth building at any price."

2003/09/23

But I Never Go Down There,
So Why Should I care?

Side Note

Like A Cave?

Some have said their crawl spaces are like caves. But since there is not rotting organic material in caves, the air quality in a cave is much better than most crawl spaces.

Many homeowners, I'd bet most, know their crawl space is nasty, so they never go down there. I don't blame them. In fact, I've never seen a dirt crawl space (that hasn't been retrofitted) where I crawled in and said "Heyyyy, this is pretty nice." I never even said, "Heyyyy, this is okay". It's always bad. Often really bad.

Homeowners know it, and don't go down into their crawl space unless they absolutely have to. They shut it out of their "often visited places in my house" list, and shut it out of their mind, like it doesn't exist. Hey, if I don't go down there, what do I care? Right? Wrong. Way wrong.

If you care about how much you pay for heating and cooling, then you care about your crawl space. If you care about your home rotting, or mold, allergies, or asthma, then you care about your crawl space. If you care about the comfort of your home, cold floors, drafts, and how your home smells, then you care about your crawl space. If you care how long the paint lasts on your house, about doors and windows sticking, about hardwood floors buckling, and about carpets going moldy, then you care about your crawl space. If you care about your resale value, then you care about your crawl space. You can't get away from it.

The house is one building. It operates as a system. You can't have one part of the building that is sick, and another part that is healthy. You can't rationalize that you never go in the crawl space so you aren't affected by it. Why? Simple. Air mixing.

Mold growing on a door upstairs from a wet summer crawl space.

10/06/2003

The crawl space air is bad. It is damp. It is cold if it's winter. It is full of mold spores. It smells. And this crawl space air is in your building envelope. It gets upstairs in one of two ways – the stack effect (explained on next page), or the HVAC system through your ducts. You are breathing it. In fact we know that $^1/_3$ to $^1/_2$ of the air that you breathe on the first floor of your house came through your crawl space. And this goes for basements too, for people who have them.

This fact has been proven by studies. If someone spray paints something in your crawl space, do you think you'd smell the spray paint upstairs? Of course you would.

Radon gas is a naturally occurring radioactive gas that comes from the ground. For many years we have known that if you measure the radon levels in your basement or crawl space, and then measure upstairs, you will have about $^1/_3$ the amount upstairs. Since radon only comes from the ground, this demonstrates how air moves in a house – from bottom to top.

3

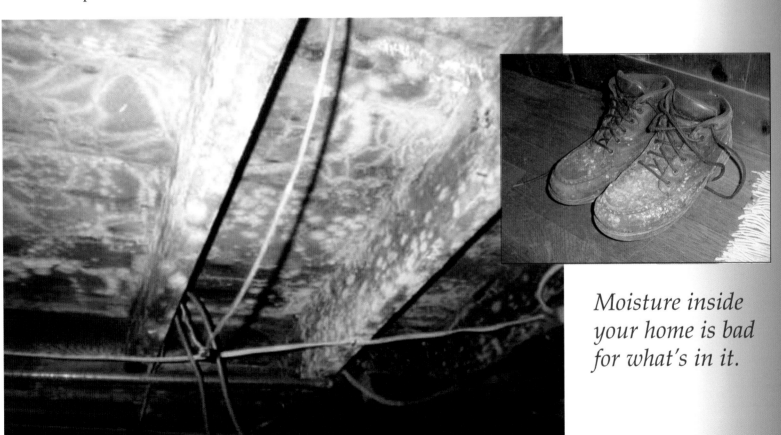

*Moisture inside
your home is bad
for what's in it.*

You Breathe Crawl Space Air—
Like it or Not

S T A C K   E F F E C T

This ★ is a **BIG** ★ IDEA!

As warm air rises in a home it leaks out of the upper levels. New air must enter to replace the air that escaped. In fact, in a tight home about half of the air escapes each hour out of the upper levels. This creates a suction at the lower levels to draw in replacement air. In older leaky homes the air exchange rate can be as high as two air exchanges per hour.

What this "stack effect" does is create an airflow in your home from bottom to top. So air from the basement is drawn upwards into the first floor, and then to the second floor. Of course it dilutes with other air in your home, but building scientists say that up to 50% of the air you breathe on the first floor is air that came from the crawl space. If you have hot air heating with ductwork, the air mixes even more thoroughly throughout the house.

Therefore, whatever is in your crawl space air is in your house and affecting you, whether you spend any time in the crawl space or not. If there is high humidity downstairs, there is higher humidity upstairs than there would be otherwise. If there is mold in the crawl space, there are mold spores upstairs. If there are damp odors in your crawl space – you get the idea.

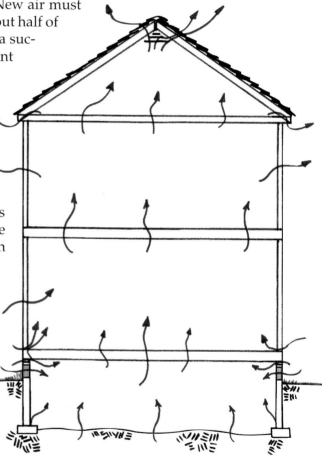

So this idea that we put in crawl space vents, and expect that air will flow in through vents on one side of the house and out through the vents on the other side is a bunch of baloney. What actually happens is air enters the vents in the front, enters the vents in the back, and enters the vents on the sides, and then it goes UP!

Some say that on a windy day the air flows through a crawl space via the vents. The problem is you need wind everyday for this to be effective. The downside is that wind depressurizes the whole building, sucking air out of it at a greater rate than it blows it in. This causes a need for more replacement air to make up for the air that left. So we suck more air up from the vented crawl space on a windy day.

Besides, even if vents made air flow through a crawl space on a windy day, you are just making warm humid air or very cold air flow through your house faster because of the wind. Venting doesn't make sense unless the outdoor air is 70 degrees and 45% RH day and night, all year long. So it doesn't make sense.

How does the air get from the crawl space up into the house (besides ducts)? Air is a very small thing. With this driving mechanism, (the suction of the house on the ground) air is drawn up through every tiny opening between the crawl space and your house. Holes around wires and pipes. Joints in floor boards, space around access hatches and through duct chases. You can seal these openings, but you can never get it perfect, so you can't stop it.

"Venting doesn't make sense unless the outdoor air is 70 degres and 45% relative humidity day and night, year round."

3

How long do you want your home to last? The vented dirt crawl space has sentenced this new home to an early demise.

Increased Energy Bills

Damp air takes more energy to cool in the summer and heat in the winter.

"Just Add Water"
Negative Effects of a Wet or Damp Crawl Space

Since air flows upward into the upper levels of your home from the crawl space, it brings the humidity from the crawl space with it. The effects on your home can include:

◆ Dust Mites (the number one indoor allergen)
◆ Sticking (swollen) doors and windows
◆ Smelly damp carpets
◆ Buckling hardwood floors
◆ Condensation/rotting/mold in your attic (as humid air escapes into your attic it can condense against the cold ceiling or roof)
◆ Frost or condensation and mold on the inside of windows in cool weather
◆ Increased cooling bills (damp air takes more energy to cool)
◆ Increased heating bills (damp air takes more energy to heat)
◆ Mold upstairs
◆ Decreased life of roof sheathing and shingles
◆ Decreased life of the paint on the outside of your house
◆ Aggravated asthma and allergies

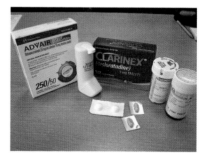

The damage in the crawl space itself is obvious. The above list represents many of the effects that can happen <u>upstairs</u> that you may not associate with your wet or damp crawl space.

3

Air Mixing Through Your Ducts

(Skip this section if you have hot water heat)

If you have ducts in your crawl space, which most do, then you have a built in air highway to efficiently mix all the air in your home – from crawl space to the upper floor. How? It's simple – duct leakage.

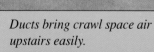

Ducts bring crawl space air upstairs easily.

D ucts are made of segments of sheet metal, or combinations of sheet metal, duct board and flex duct. Between the sections and at the elbows there are joints which are simply bent, crimped or screwed together.

Supply ducts are under pressure, blowing the air that you pay to heat and cool from your heating and cooling equipment to the rooms you want to heat and cool. As this pressurized air passes by loose joints and seams in the duct, a little air leaks out. Okay, so it's only 2% of the air in the duct. No biggie, right? Well what about the next joint? 2% of the <u>remaining</u> air leaks out. And the next, and the next? It adds up. When you have a lot of supply duct leakage, a couple things happen. You depressurize the living spaces above and pressurize the crawl space. This pushes the damp, smelly, moldy air from the crawl space up into the living spaces faster than it would move in that direction otherwise. It's a no win situation. It costs you money and you and your family breathe diluted crawl space air all day.

Return ducts suck air from the rooms you want to heat and cool, to the heating/cooling unit. They run through the crawl space, and when they leak, they suck in the bad air from the crawl space directly into your duct system and blow it right back into the house. So that's a losing situation too.

The average home with ducts has 300 cubic feet per minute of duct leakage. One possible solution is to seal the ducts. Before you do, you should finish reading this book, because your crawl space and the bad effects it has on your house can be fixed without doing this.

Sealed duct systems do exist, but you have a better chance of seeing "Bigfoot". A contractor would use duct mastic (not duct tape, which is good for everything except sealing ducts) and paint the stuff on every joint in the duct system. An arduous process indeed, especially when lying on your back in mud, with spider webs in your hair.

"If that's on the outside of the duct, what's on the inside?"

3

Ducts in a Dirt Crawl Space –
More Bad News

When warm humid air enters crawl space vents, where is the first place it will give up its moisture? On the coldest surfaces, right? The coldest surface is likely to be your ducts when the air conditioning is on. Water is a conductor, not an insulator. So when a duct is wet, it is warmed by the summer air that came through the crawl space vents.

A friend of mine, Royce Lewis, at Comfort Diagnostics in Little Rock, Arkansas measured the air coming out of an air conditioning unit at 55 degrees. Then he measured the temperature at the other end of the duct line where the vent came into the room – and the air was 65 degrees! The AC unit was cooling the air by 20 degrees – from 75 degrees to 55 degrees – but the air was back up to 65 degrees by the time it got back into the room! That's a full 50% energy loss! Why? The duct was wet and running through a warmer space.

Here's more bad news for those of you who heat your homes. You wouldn't purify water and send it through dirty pipes before you drink it, right? Yet we heat our air and send it through cold ducts to our rooms. The ducts are thin sheet metal, sometimes with thin insulation, most of the times not. We have open vents in our crawl space and it's 30 degrees out. So the ducts are cold. You lose again. I know it's disheartening and frustrating, but there is a solution. Read on.

Ducts that are wet from condensation rob you of energy.

Higher Energy Bills
From Your Dirt Crawl Space

Important to Save Energy

A home with a dirt crawl space costs more to heat and cool. Besides all the reasons we already mentioned, there are other factors working against you. If your crawl space is vented, those vents make your floors cold upstairs. This is not only uncomfortable, but it costs more to heat your house.

Houses with dirt crawl spaces have damp air. Damp air uses more energy to heat and cool, and this costs more money. Damp air puts more of a "latent" (hidden) load on the HVAC system. Everyone knows they need to run their AC more on a humid day. But what about humidity from inside the building? Same thing. If you get rid of the humidity from your crawl space, you save money on heating and cooling costs.

How much money? You will save 15% to 25%! That's a lot of money! Over the years, it really adds up! You are paying the price each and every month in higher energy bills, by living in a house with a dirt crawl space. Of course there are vari-ables, such as how many vents you have, whether you live in a one or two story home, if you have ducts in the crawl space, how big your crawl space is, etc.

These penalties from living with, and the savings from fixing the dirt crawl space problem are real and proven. Advanced Energy, a private non-profit organiza-tion funded by both public and private funds, has done studies to measure these effects.

Dirt crawl spaces make the air in your house damp, and damp air costs more to heat and cool.

Fixing your crawl space is one home repair you can't afford not to make

3

Important   Important to
              Save Energy

3   If light can get in, so can air.

With the lights off you can see sunlight around this crawl space access door. Air leaks like this where outside air can enter a crawl space must be sealed to get control of the indoor environment.

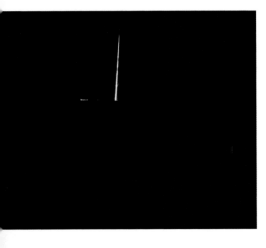

Crawlspace RH (Summer 2002)

Relative Humidity (%)

100, 90, 80, 70, 60, 50

6/3   6/13   6/23   7/3   7/13   7/23   8/2   8/12   8/22   9/1

—— **Outside**   —— **Vented Crawl Spaces**   —— **Sealed Vents**

Advanced Energy compared the Relative Humidity in sealed unvented crawl spaces to the RH in vented dirt crawl spaces and the RH outdoors. This chart clearly shows that sealed unvented crawl spaces have far less moisture in them, ending any lingering debate on the venting issue.

In fact, the energy loss is so substantial in a home with a vented dirt crawl space with ducts, that you may as well ignore all other ways to save energy and make your home more comfortable until you fix the crawl space problem. Caulking around a window, or weather-stripping a door, would be like patching a tiny hole in a rowboat, and ignoring the foot-wide hole on the other side.

Controlling air infiltration is the key to energy conservation in a building. Closing up those giant holes in your crawl space walls, and eliminating the "reason" (exposed damp earth) why they were there in the first place must be top priority. **Important**

In one Advanced Energy study, the organization experimented with 12 identical new homes in a Habitat for Humanity subdivision. Some of the homes had vented dirt crawl spaces, and others were sealed, much like we will recommend in this book. By sub-metering the heat pumps, they found that the homes with the vented dirt crawl spaces cost $28 more to cool <u>in a single month!</u> (June 2003). But there are a few catches.

First, the homes were small. If the homes were twice as big, we might expect twice as many dollars saved in energy costs. Second, the ones with a "vented dirt crawl space" had two things going for them that the average house with vented dirt crawl spaces does not. They had a 6 mil plastic ground cover down on the floor, and they had their ducts sealed. In a 100 house study in 1994, Advanced Energy determined that the average house has more than 300 cubic feet per minute of duct leakage of which these comparison homes did not have.

If this control group of houses was more like the millions of real homes across the country we see out there, the difference in energy use would be even more dramatic.

Nevertheless, it doesn't take long before the numbers add up to serious money. Add to that the benefits of preserving your home's value and eliminating rot repairs and mold remediation, and you see that fixing your crawl space is one home repair you can't afford not to make.

Spread across the 26 million homes with dirt crawl spaces, it is estimated that with just a 15% energy savings, homeowners in the U.S. alone would save 7 billion dollars annually! That's a lot of money that could be better spent somewhere else.

This is a **BIG** IDEA!

Important to Save Energy

Important

Sealing Vents

Basement Systems Inc. has developed permanent gasketed vent covers to stop unwanted outside air.

3

VENT COVERS

The CleanSpace® Vent Cover seals crawl space vents permanently from the outside to stop unwanted outside air from entering the crawl space, while covering ugly vents with an attractive panel. The available colors of black, gray and red brick match a home's foundation nicely.

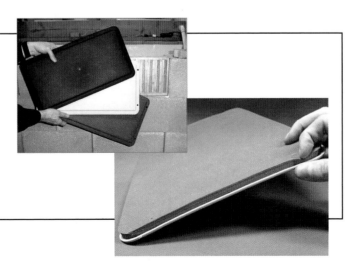

"An insulation diaper"

3

The plastic facing on this insulation prevents it from drying. It gets heavy and droops down making an air space between it and the floor. It has almost no thermal benefit at all. This is common with paper and foil faced insulation as well.

Insulation Myths

Some crawl spaces have insulation in the floor above, and some do not. A few important points need to be made. First, one reason for insulation in the floor above is that the crawl space is so cold in the winter due to the open vents. These vents should be closed permanently which would make a huge difference in the temperature of the floor above.

Mold loves paper facing on insulation.

Important to Save Energy

Second, fiberglass insulation only works in a closed cavity. Fiberglass insulation is loose and air passes right through it. When it is between the joists in a vented crawl space, with the paper or foil side up, and the unfaced side down, it's not doing much at all.

Another thing about the facing is that paper-faced insulation is "mold candy"- a term I borrow from Joe Lstiburek from Building Science Corp. Mold loves paper even more than wood.

Foil-faced insulation is supposed to be a radiant barrier. You put the foil face to the heated side. But you need to have at least a $\frac{1}{2}$" air space in front of foil radiant barriers for them to reflect the heat. All the insulation I see, if it has a radiant barrier, is jammed up against the floor sheathing with no air space between the radiant barrier and the sheathing. Therefore, that element of the insulation is

not working. Besides, such an air space creates a thermal bypass where air can flow on both sides of the insulation, rendering the insulation useless.

Mold grows on insulation because it has some organic material in the resin used to set the fibers. A last important note, is that when fiberglass insulation is just a little damp, it loses a whole lot of its insulation value.

So what is your fiberglass insulation doing in your dirt crawl space? Not much.

Insulation and moisture: a very bad combination.

Insulating is still a good idea. If you do it, insulate the crawl space walls along with your crawl space solution (keep reading) and use foam insulation. This can be rigid foam boards or, even better, sprayed closed cell foam. A plumbing leak is bound to happen one day and I want insulation that won't get ruined and support mold growth. Another good alternative is a radiant barrier on your walls to reflect interior heat back into the crawl space.

Any foam insulation used must meet the ASTM 84E standard for a flame spread of 25 or less and smoke density of 450 or less. If not, it must be covered by another material – which is not practical! In general, white styrofoam beadboard does not meet the standard, but pink or blue foam boards do. If any inspector is not happy with pink or blue board, you can use Dow Thermax – a polyisocyanurate foam board with foil on both sides.

The primary focus of this book is to control moisture (and mold and rot) and achieve gross energy savings by closing vents and stopping unconditioned air from leaking into a crawl space, notwithstanding insulation.

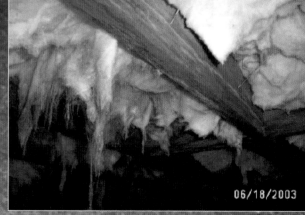

06/18/2003

Fiberglass insulation does little when it's either not in a closed cavity or when it's damp, like this.

Chapter 4

Back to the Earth –
Mold, Fungus and Rot

Mold has become a big issue in recent years. Mold is the subject of lawsuits, a terror to builders, subject matter for front-page writers, the reason for school closings, and the growth of a "new" industry – mold testing and remediation. With all this talk about mold, you might think it is new. It is not new. You might think it is a complex issue. It is not a complex issue, but rather very simple.

First, let's talk about why mold is here in the first place. Mold has a purpose. Its purpose is to breakdown or eat dead organic matter. That's what God put it here for. Without mold, plant and animal material would grow and grow and pile up and pile up.

Important

06/18/2003

06/18/2003

Wet load bearing girders and floor joists under attack by mold. Soon this framing will get so rotted, it will all need to be replaced.

"Mold Intelligence"

Mold knows why it was put here. If it's organic, dead, and wet, mold knows to eat it. Organic means it is a material that was once living, such as wood. Mold sends out its spores everywhere, which can lay dormant for many years. So when something is organic, dead and wet, mold grows on it and eats it. When we say "mold", we mean any mold or other fungi, of which there are many thousands of varieties.

No laughing matter- It's just a matter of time before a damp crawl space rots your floor out.

Since mold spores are everywhere, and our building materials and contents of our homes (furniture, boxes, clothes, etc.) are made from organic materials, this factor cannot be controlled. The only one that we can control in our homes is the moisture.

Mold needs 70% Relative Humidity (RH) to grow; however this is a loose number. Some molds can grow at less RH. In many cases, like in a crawl space, the RH of the surrounding air, and the RH of the surfaces are two different things because of temperature differences between air and surfaces.

Mold likes processed organic fibers best— it will grow on paper and cardboard first. Paper is like "mold candy". After that it will grow on fiberboard and chipboard, and then plywood, and finally on framing lumber. Sheetrock has paper on it. Mold loves sheetrock.

Mold releases airborne spores or "seeds", which are so light they float on the slightest air currents, off to find more suitable places to grow. Most people are not allergic to mold spores, but some are. The higher the concentration of mold spores, the greater percentage of people who will be bothered by them.

There is plenty of information out there on the health effects of mold, and they will not be explained here. One thing is for sure; mold growing in your house is not good. It's not good for your health, and it is increasingly not good for your property value. Who wants to buy a house with mold? Nobody.

The sill plate rotting right over this vent is no coincidence. That the problem wasn't fixed after the wood was replaced is the irony.

Look at the pretty flowers Mommy! ▶
▼

Damp Leather— Sound the mold ▶ *dinner bell!*

To Your Health
(And if not yours, then theirs)

You can't find a doctor who says mold in a home is good. You can't find a doctor who says mold in your home is "not bad." It's bad. It's all bad.

Besides irritating people with asthma and mold allergies, studies show that prolonged exposure to mold can actually cause asthma.

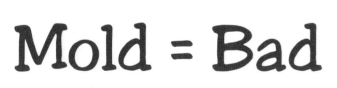

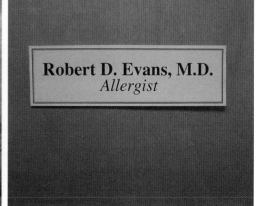

Robert D. Evans, M.D.
Allergist

There is another industry that has vented dirt crawl spaces to thank for its existence – Structural repairs to replace floor joists, girders, and sill plates – basically the entire floor framing system under your house. These repairs aren't cheap. In fact, they can be very expensive. You can imagine a carpenter figuring out how he's going to crawl under your home and get new 16 foot long 2" x 10"s in place, with all the duct work, wiring, plumbing, and bridging (cross bracing) that are attached to the old rotted joists, all while operating on his back in a low crawl space. It's not easy on him, and it's not going to be easy on your bank account.

Most of the time, these structural repairs are done without ever fixing the problem! So it's only a matter of time before the new framing rots out, and it has to be done again.

What is the design life of a house? In other words, how long do you want your house to last without needing major repairs? If the answer is longer than 10 or 15 or 25 years, then you better fix your dirt crawl space.

When you look at the cost of higher energy bills, and especially when you add that year's pro rata share of rot repairs when they eventually will have to be done, you can easily see that it is more expensive to live with a dirt crawl space than to fix it right now. By not fixing your dirt crawl space, over the life of the house, you are paying many times more than it costs to fix now.

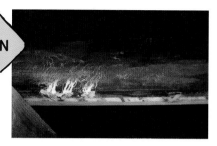

When the floors in nearly all 36 units in this New England condominium complex began bouncing and getting soft, they realized the crawl spaces were a bigger problem than they thought. As an emergency measure, they had to "sister" new framing lumber to each side of every girder and every floor joist so the homes would not cave in. Eventually they hired Basement Systems to install a CleanSpace® Crawl Space Encapsulation™ system to fix the moisture problem.

CAUTION

"Meet Your Sister"

The practice of nailing a new floor joist alongside a structurally compromised old one is called "sistering." This is done because the subfloor above and utilities etc. are nailed to the old joist, so it's nearly impossible to remove.

Sistering may restore structural strength to the joist, but it leaves the old rotting joist in place. And soon, the sister will get moldy too. And what about the rotted plywood subfloor above? Without fixing the real problem – Moisture – I can't see how many homes won't be condemned in the future. What do you think?

4

No Joke

These joists appear to melt into a softening sill plate as they rot — And termites love wet wood. You can see the remnants of a termite tunnel up the wall here in this photo.

Important

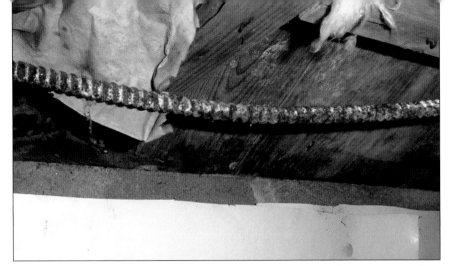

When BX cable rusts out, the electrical ground is lost – a very dangerous situation.

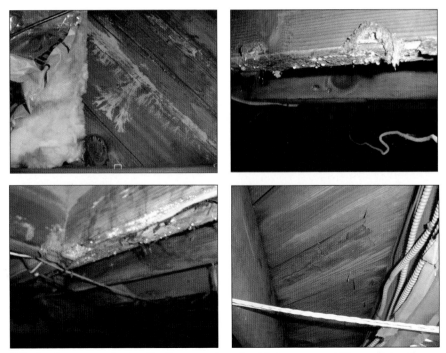

What's cheaper, replacing the floors and paying higher energy bills, or fixing the dirt crawl space? Answer: Fixing your dirt crawl space.

4

Dust Mites and Other Critters
Love Your Dirt Crawl Space

The number one allergen that people with asthma and allergies react to is dust mite droppings. Dust mites are microscopic parasites that live off of skin flakes that you shed. They live in your bedding, your carpet, and your furniture. Dust Mite droppings are tiny and float in the air, where they can be breathed in and aggravate allergies and asthma. For more excellent, easy to understand information, visit www.housedustmite.org.

Dust mites do not drink water, but instead absorb water from the air. They need over 50% Relative Humidity to live. While dust mites do not live in your crawl space, they like your crawl space. Why? It is very difficult to keep your house dry when you have a dirt crawl space under it, and it's this life giving humidity that allows dust mites to thrive upstairs. Dry the crawl space out, and the air flowing up into the house is no longer wet, so the house dries out. The dust mites, which are like tiny water balloons, dry out and die, and of course, stop pooping. That's great news for allergy and asthma sufferers.

Other pests love the moisture in the crawl space too. Termites love wet wood. Spiders love crawl spaces because they eat other bugs, and there are usually plenty of them in a nice damp dirt crawl space. Mice and rats like dirt crawl spaces, and snakes, and all kinds of critters and creatures think a crawl space is a nice place too. And when it's time to die, a dirt crawl space is often a nice peaceful place to do that – and subsequently decompose. Blessed are crawl space workers who can go in and do their job without being creeped out too bad!

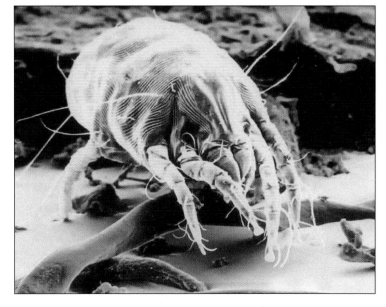

Dust mites live upstairs and thrive in humid environments. Dust mite droppings are the number one indoor allergen.

4

Bugs love your dirt crawl space!

4

Mice are very happy to live and die in your dirt crawl space.

What's that White Chalky Powder?

Efflorescence is from minerals in the concrete, mortar, or soil that dissolve in water and remain behind when the water evaporates off the surface of the wall or floor. It appears as white powder or crystals. It is sometimes confused with mold, but it is not alive – just mineral residue. It is not harmful unless you eat it and can be swept or brushed off. It is a sign that water is (probably, slowly) coming through the concrete.

That White Chalky Powder on Your Walls is Effloresence

4

SOLUTIONS

The dirt crawl space problem is one where you get a whole lot of benefit by fixing it, without having a terribly expensive and disruptive home improvement project to deal with.

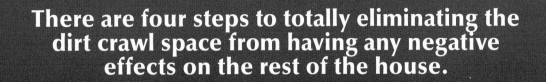

There are four steps to totally eliminating the dirt crawl space from having any negative effects on the rest of the house.

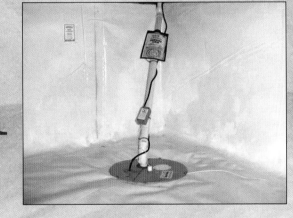

1

Step one - Fix the water leakage (if there is any.)

3

Step three - Seal the vents and other outside air leaks.

2

Step two - Isolate the house from the earth.

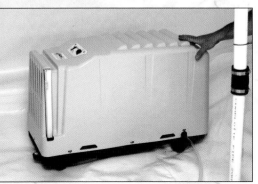

4

Step four - "Condition" or dehumidify your crawl space air.

Chapter 5

Step One: Fixing the Groundwater Leakage

Some crawl spaces don't leak when it rains hard. If this is you, go to step two. If your crawl space does leak when it rains hard, even if it's only once in a while, then you have to do something to control the groundwater before you isolate your home from the earth with the CleanSpace Encapsulation System.

If you don't know if your crawl space leaks, do a careful inspection to look for signs of water pooling in the low areas. Most crawl spaces have a lowest spot, or perhaps several areas that are lower than the rest. Look in these areas carefully with a good light. If water ponds there, even if it's only once every few years when it gets really wet outside, you will see signs of that happening. Look for waterlines, rings of silt and fine soil particles that washed down to the low areas, or erosion patterns in the soil where the water made its way from its entry point to the low spot. I have seen crawl spaces that leak very badly, getting up to a foot of water in a space that is only 24" high to begin with! Others are much more mild.

Standing water needs to be addressed prior to the installation of CleanSpace.

The first thing that must be done is the installation of a sump pump. To install one, a hole must be dug that is 22" deep and at least as wide at the low spot of the crawl space. The soil can be removed or spread around in the crawl space to fill other low areas, or to crown the middle a bit. The idea is to have the crawl space floor pitch down, even if only slightly, towards the sump hole, and not have other low areas where water can puddle before it gets to the sump hole.

The next thing to do is install a sump liner in the hole to keep the mud out, providing a nice housing for the pump. A specially designed crawl space sump system has features such as:

1. A sturdy liner made to mate with a lid.
2. An airtight lid.
3. A floor drain in the lid in case of a plumbing leak.
4. A reliable cast-iron pump with mechanical float switch.
5. A stand under the pump.
6. An alarm to alert you to pump failure or a plumbing leak.

Open sump holes like this are useless in stopping water vapor from rising from the ground.

Some crawl spaces exist because there is rock ledge that the builder did not have the means or desire to remove to dig a basement. In some cases with rock ledge you cannot get a sump hole 22″ deep and have to settle for as deep as you can get; 10″ being an absolute minimum.

The sump liner should be sturdy, and have lots of holes in it to allow water from the ground to enter and be pumped out. It should also accept an airtight lid.

A sump lid that is sturdy and airtight is very important because you are trying to dry the crawl space out completely. You don't want an open hole with water sitting in it, to evaporate up into your crawl space environment.

The pump is next. I recommend a pump that is $1/3$ hp, cast iron, and that has a mechanical float switch. Pumps with pressure switches or "ball on a wire switches" should be avoided. A check valve should be installed on the discharge line very close to the pump. The discharge pipe should be $1\frac{1}{2}$″ PVC pipe and run to the exterior of the house.

A proper discharge line location will vary from property to property. The idea is to get the water to run to a place in the yard where it will continue its flow downhill and away from the house once it comes out of the discharge line. If you have good pitch away from your house then you may not need to run it very far. If your yard is relatively flat, then you may have to run it farther. We have run discharge lines from 3 to 103 feet away from a foundation, with 15 feet as an average.

Some pumps don't run very often and it's not a big issue, and others run quite often. The good news is that you can always extend or move the sump discharge location later if the first location proves to be unsuitable.

A "Super" Sump

A high quality sump system is essential and must include a perforated sump liner, reliable pump, alarm system, pump stand, check valve, and an airtight lid with a floor drain. Shown here is Basement Systems' SuperSump system.

cutaway view

5

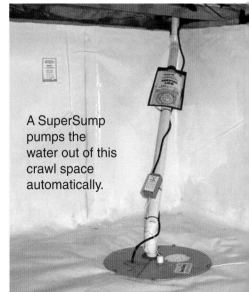
A SuperSump pumps the water out of this crawl space automatically.

There are a few other important elements to a proper sump installation in your crawl space.

Important

A Stand for the Pump

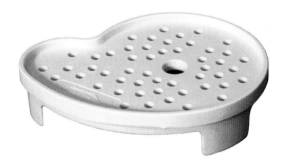

A "CleanPump Stand" will elevate the pump off the bottom of the sump liner a bit, allowing for some sediment, mud, debris, or gravel that washes into the sump liner to settle to the bottom of the sump liner without clogging or otherwise affecting the pump. It also keeps the check valve and discharge pipe clean. A check valve (one-way valve) should be installed on all sump pump discharge lines, so when the pump shuts off the water in the pipe doesn't flow back into the sump hole, which would then have to be pumped again on the next cycle.

5 | Pump Alarms

How would you know if your sump pump has failed and you were in danger of being flooded? Unless you have an alarm, the answer is, when your crawl space is already flooded, which is just what you are trying to avoid. A battery powered alarm that sounds off automatically when the water reaches a level above the point where the pump(s) should normally turn on is essential. The patented WaterWatch alarm does just that, telling you there is a problem before the floor gets wet, giving you a chance to do something about it.

Important

Provide for Plumbing Leaks

However, you must account for plumbing leaks. This sump installation is only part of the solution to your problem, and will be installed along with the crawl space liner. Not if, but when you have a plumbing leak, you don't want your plastic-lined crawl space to fill with water, like a swimming pool, but you want it to go down into the sump hole instead. The problem is the sump has an airtight lid on it. The solution? – a floor drain in the airtight lid that lets water go down but doesn't let damp air rise.

48

M any crawl spaces I have worked in have plumbing leaks that the home owner never realized, because the water was soaking into the dirt floor. After we install our CleanSpace lining (which we will discuss later) in their crawl space we see the drips on top of it, and tell them about it so they can get a plumber in to fix the leak.

If you don't need a sump pump in your crawl space, a SmartDrain alarm and drain unit should be installed. [See page 61 for more information.]

Our Basement Systems' "SuperSump" has all the components specifically designed to meet all the important criteria detailed here.

Once the sump liner is installed, the space between the sump liner and the hole in the ground is filled to the top with clean stone aggregate. This "stone zone" allows water from the surface of the dirt (under your crawl space liner which is the next step) to drain down into it and through the holes in the sump liner to be pumped out.

A Smart Drain. *Basement Systems' SmartDrain warns of interior leaks.*

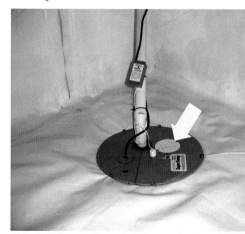
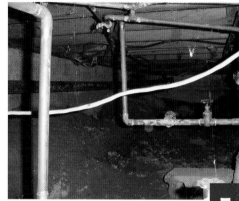

Plumbing Leak Protection

Water from future plumbing leaks must be considered – it will happen one day.

5

"One Way." *An air-tight sump lid with a drain keeps water vapor sealed in, while allowing water to drain down in the event of a plumbing leak.*

![!] This ⭐BIG⭐ is a IDEA! **What if my pump fails? What if the power goes out?**

Important

These are questions you should be asking yourself. After all, if you want your crawl space dry ALL the time, you're not going to get it if you don't plan on...

❖ The power going out one day – which usually happens in a big storm with rain
❖ The circuit breaker tripping
❖ The primary pump failing
❖ The primary pump not being able to keep up with the amount of water in a very heavy rain
❖ The pump coming unplugged

Remember all the stories of woe people have told you about the sump pump failing and them getting flooded? These are the reasons they were talking about. You don't have to go through that if you get the right equipment.

Is a Generator an Option?

A generator is a good idea if you have an automatic one permanently installed that senses when the power goes out and starts up automatically. It needs to be wired by an electrician. A typical generator can be hooked up to run your sump pump, a few lights, the furnace, and the fridge. This costs between $7,000 to $10,000 in most cases. If you go this route, be sure to install two AC primary pumps to cover you in case of pump failure, as a generator only eliminates the need for the DC back-up pump.

You can purchase a portable generator for $400 or so. However you have to be home (and awake) to notice when the power fails. Then you have to drag the

generator outside, gas it up, start it up, and run an extension cord to your sump pump. This is not a good option.

Unless you have an automatic generator for back-up power in your home, a battery back-up sump pump system such as our "UltraSump" system is highly recommended. This system includes a second DC operated pump, a second switch, a special long term standby battery, and a matched smart charging system and control unit. If the water rises above the point where the primary pump should turn on for any reason, including a power outage, then the secondary pumping system will automatically operate to pump the water out. In addition, there is an alarm that alerts you that the pump is running on battery power, so if there is a malfunction with the primary pump, or there is no power to the primary pump, you have time to get the primary pump going again before the battery goes dead.

AC/DC

AC = (Alternating Current) plugged into the wall – runs off house power
DC = (Direct Current) Runs off battery power

In many crawl spaces, probably most, the pump will be all the drainage you need before going to step two, where you install a crawl space liner. This depends on the grade in your crawl space. Remember that the water comes in at the perimeter of the crawl space. We don't need to keep the dirt floor dry, like we would need to keep a basement floor dry if we were waterproofing a basement. We just need to keep the water from puddling, and allow it to run to the sump location. If we can regrade with a small rake or hoe to make paths for the water to flow to the sump location, then that's fine.

Basement Systems' SuperSump with an UltraSump

cutaway view

A battery back-up pumping system *automatically pumps the water out in the event of a power failure, or a pump failure, or if the pump is unplugged or the circuit breaker trips.*

A nother option is to dig a shallow trench at the perimeter to make the water flow to the sump location. In extreme cases you can dig a deeper trench and install a perforated PVC drainage pipe, and even add stone around it – but in most cases this is a waste of resources and not necessary to accomplish what you need to.

Besides the water, you _must_ remove the water vapor.

Sump Pump Discharge Lines

Terminating the discharge line in your yard can be done in a variety of ways, but in most cases is best accomplished with a "LawnScape Outlet." This durable fitting diffuses the discharge water while camouflaging the end of the pipe.

5

No Dice. *Someone thought that a drainage trench was a good idea in this crawl space, but without a completely sealed encapsulation system to encapsulate the dirt and separate the house from the earth, it did nothing to solve the moisture problem.*

Water Vapor Needs to be Addressed. *Some crawl spaces have a layer of gravel on the dirt floor. This does nothing to stop the water vapor from rising into the house. These homes will need a sealed liner encapsulation system.*

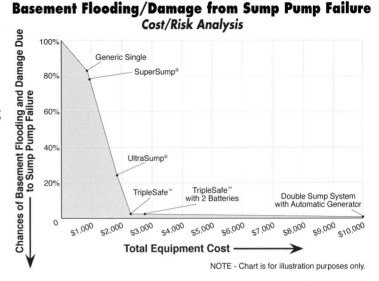

Basement Flooding/Damage from Sump Pump Failure
Cost/Risk Analysis

Chances of Basement Flooding and Damage Due to Sump Pump Failure (vertical axis: 0, 20%, 40%, 60%, 80%, 100%)

Generic Single

SuperSump®

UltraSump®

TripleSafe™

TripleSafe™ with 2 Batteries

Double Sump System with Automatic Generator

Total Equipment Cost → ($1,000, $2,000, $3,000, $4,000, $5,000, $6,000, $7,000, $8,000, $9,000, $10,000)

NOTE - Chart is for illustration purposes only.

For Those with Zero Tolerance for Crawl Space Water

To reduce your chances of getting flooded from pump failure down to a statistically insignificant number, you'll need the best sump pumping system available.

The answer is a system called the "TripleSafe" sump pump system. This top-of-the-line system sports three sump pumps in one sump liner. Pump 1 is a high-quality Zoeller 1/3 hp pump and will do the lion's share of the pumping very efficiently most of the time.

Pump two is a 1/2 hp Zoeller pump set a bit higher in the sump hole that turns on in the event that the first pump can't keep up or if it fails. This second pump is more powerful and has a separate discharge line to give you that "turbo boost" in those rare cases that you need it.

Pump 3 is an "UltraSump," DC (battery-operated) pump that kicks in if the power goes out. It is available with one or two specially designed batteries to pump out over 8,000 or over 16,000 gallons of water respectively.

▲ *A crawl space fitted with the CleanSpace System, a TripleSafe Pumping System, and a SaniDry Air System.*

5

Side Note

1+1=1

If you have more than one AC pump to get more water out in a big rain, it makes no sense to hook them up to one discharge pipe. Using the "Ten pounds of stuff in a five pound bag" logic, you can't get more water out with two pumps unless you have two discharge pipes to the outside.

The TripleSafe twin liner, lids, CleanPump Stands, bridge, etc., are all specially engineered to work together.

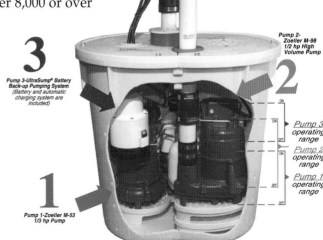

3 Pump 3-UltraSump® Battery Back-up Pumping System (Battery and automatic charging system are included)

2 Pump 2-Zoeller M-98 1/2 hp High Volume Pump

Pump 3 operating range

Pump 2 operating range

Pump 1 operating range

1 Pump 1-Zoeller M-53 1/3 hp Pump

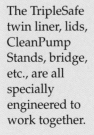

If it doesn't snow in the winter where you are, skip this.

!

CAUTION – Winter can be hazardous to your crawl space's health.

Important

Freezing Discharge Lines

Your sump pump gets the water out of the crawl space and away from your house with a pipe – usually plastic and usually about $1^1/_2$ inches in diameter. This pipe runs on the surface of the ground or in a shallow buried trench and discharges the water onto the surface away from the house.

The problem is that in winter the outlet of the pipe becomes blocked with snow and ice. When the pump runs, it fills the pipe with water. (Ten feet of $1^1/_2$-inch pipe holds one gallon of water). Since the water can't get out of the pipe due to the ice at the outlet, the whole pipe fills with water and freezes. Now your pump runs, but cannot get the water out, and your crawl space floods. Just what you were trying to avoid!

Basement Systems has a solution – The IceGuard system. This is a specially engineered fitting that goes outside your home and automatically ejects the water away from the exterior wall in the event that the pipe freezes. It is designed with holes in it to allow this to happen, yet no water at all gets out of these openings when the pipe is not frozen.

Snow, no problem. *The patented IceGuard solves the problem of frozen discharge lines.*

With a TripleSafe pump system, both discharge lines are protected by the IceGuard sump pump discharge line system.

5

Side Note

Electrical Outlets

Electrical Outlets are usually not included in the scope of work by your waterproofing contractor. Although your waterproofer will leave with your sumps operational, plan on having a electrician wire a proper outlet at the sump location after the waterproofer is done.

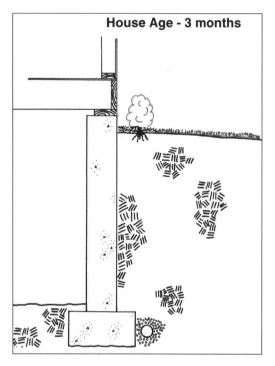

Dirt Around a Foundation Settles

When the loose soil is pushed back against a new foundation, it will settle – especially in the first few years. This doesn't help a wet crawl space situation, and dirt should be added so water does not flow toward the foundation. Unlike dirt, mulch is porous and water easily passes through it, so mulch doesn't count.

Janesky's First Law of Hydrodynamics –

Water flows downhill.

House Age - 3 months

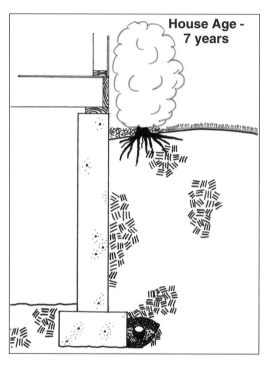

House Age - 7 years

Grading

   If the soil around your foundation is pitched toward the foundation, it's a good idea to add dirt so that the soil slopes away. Be sure not to use sand or mulch, because water flows right down through these materials whether they are pitched or not. It's best to use clay or other dense dirt.

   Be sure that you keep the dirt at least four inches down from the siding though. If the siding is close or touching the soil, it will rot and you'll have another problem. Termites could also create a highway into your home undetected.

CAUTION
Don't rely on grading alone to keep your crawl space dry.

5

54

Downspouts

You didn't need to read a book to have someone tell you to keep your gutters from dumping water next to your foundation did you? I only have to say it so someone doesn't say my book is incomplete without this obvious advice.

So how do you do it? There are a few options to laying ugly pipes and contraptions across your lawn that get in the way of mowing and your annual croquet game at the family picnic.

One way is to bury pipes from the downspouts underground away from the foundation. Rather than having an ugly pipe sticking out in your yard, the pipes can be terminated on the surface with a durable, dark green colored water dispersion

Unsightly Tripping Hazard

RainChute

LawnScape Outlet

fitting called a LawnScape Outlet. The cover unscrews to enable the removal of any debris that may collect inside.

There are a few other options that work very well. A product called RainChute is recessed into the ground just an inch or so and takes the water up to 7 feet away. Usually this is all you need to make a big difference. The advantage of RainChute is that it is not above ground to cause a tripping or mowing problem and be unsightly, yet it is not underground either so it's not expensive and won't clog.

RainChute EZ

For areas that are landscaped and don't need mowing, a simple extension called RainChute EZ will do the trick.

Gutters

Keep your gutters clean. There are a variety of gutter screening and cover materials that work well to keep them clean.

5

Don't rely on clean gutters alone to keep your crawl space dry!

Chapter 6

Step Two:
Isolate the House from the Earth

You'll Love This!

This is a BIG IDEA!

This step is the key to solving your dirt crawl space problem. This is where you turn your nasty crawl space into a nice crawl space!

There are a few criteria to deciding which approach to use. The solution must—

1. Stop water vapor from flowing up from the soil
2. Stop water vapor from flowing through or off of the crawl space walls
3. Allow water to drain from the walls to the sump location
4. Allow water to drain from the floor to the sump location
5. Not get ruined when someone crawls on it
6. Be durable, so it lasts as long as the house does
7. Be affordable

Bonus 8.   Be treated with an anti-microbial ingredient so mold and bacteria will not grow on it.

There are two basic approaches – a concrete floor and a plastic liner.

Concrete Floors

If you pour concrete in your crawl space, you have accomplished two of our criteria – the concrete won't get ruined when someone crawls on it and it will last. However, the concrete doesn't allow water from the walls or floor to drain to the sump location, and it doesn't stop water vapor from the walls or floor. In fact, water vapor goes right through concrete; especially a thin layer of concrete, which might be installed in a crawl space.

You can solve these problems. First, to stop water vapor from the floor, you'll have to lay down a vapor barrier of at least 6 mils thick before pouring the floor. The vapor barrier stops the moisture, and the concrete makes it durable. But then we have to do something to let water flow under it. We'll have to put down a layer of clean stone or gravel before our vapor barrier and concrete.

We need to drain our walls. Crawl space walls are usually made of concrete block and they leak readily. We can put plastic on the walls, but plastic such as 6 mil plastic is difficult to attach permanently to the walls, and is not durable. One solution is to run the plastic from the floor up the walls and attach a wire mesh to the wall over the plastic. Then a stucco coat of concrete can be applied to the walls, before the floor is poured.

Concrete is heavy, and mixing enough by yourself to cover your entire crawl space floor and walls is out of the question. To pour a floor 3" thick over a 1500 square foot crawl space floor alone is 14.4 cubic yards (30,000 pounds) of concrete. That is $1^1/_2$ truckloads from a concrete truck. Getting concrete from a truck into your crawl space is a whole different matter. You usually can't drag the heavy stuff to the back recesses of your crawl space in buckets fast enough before it hardens.

Getting a concrete pump is an option. The concrete truck dumps concrete into a trailer-mounted pump, which pumps it through a hose into your crawl space, where workers can spread it out as best they can. I would caution that concrete is caustic and can cause severe burns. I have seen an unwary worker emerge from a crawl space where he was kneeling and sloshing around in wet concrete for a few hours trying to get the job done. He wound up with severe chemical skin burns on his legs, arms and sides.

Trying to figure out solutions to all the challenges of fixing a crawl space with concrete, one company tries to mix Portland cement with vermiculite to make it lighter. Concrete is usually made of Portland cement, sand, stone and water. The

Concrete floors, unless combined with ways to drain the walls and floor, and ways to stop the water vapor from the walls and floor, are not the answer.

Important — This is a BIG IDEA!

How Many Times is Enough?

One ideal I try to live by is this – if we want the house to last for over 100 years, then anything we put on it or in it to protect it should last as long. Otherwise, we'll have to do the same job again in the future. Thin polyethylene film doesn't cut it.

mixture of vermiculite, which may be best described to a layperson as "natural Styrofoam beads", and Portland cement makes for a weak final product, which you can feel your kneecaps push into when you crawl on it. Some vermiculite, from a mine that has now been closed, has asbestos in it.

When any concrete is pumped into a crawl space, there is a strong urge to add extra water to the mix to make it flow easier. This however, weakens the concrete, and makes it crack as it dries. Further, you have no chance of getting loose concrete to stay up on crawl space walls.

While you can make concrete work as a crawl space solution, the cost and challenges of preparing for it, and placing it make it hard to argue that it's the best option. There is a better way.

This home had a 6 mil polyethylene ground cover, but because it had holes in it and it wasn't sealed at the perimeter up the walls, and because the vents were left open, the house rotted anyway.

Plastic Liners

In the past, it has been popular to lay down thin plastic such as 6 mil thin plastic on crawl space floors. In fact the building code has allowed it as an option to cut the venting requirement by 90% if it is done. But thin plastic does not meet our criteria that the solution must not get ruined when somebody crawls on it, and must last as long as the house does. Six mil polyethylene easily rips, and gets holes poked in it when you crawl on it. Further, it is very difficult to attach to walls, and can be easily pulled down.

The researchers at Advanced Energy found that while it held the moisture down okay, they encourage thicker, stronger materials due to poor durability. Other contractors and homeowners report that 6 mil poly must be repaired all the time because of holes and rips that occur after they go in the crawl space. One said he has ripped holes in it with his belt buckle and cell phone antennae.

Can you believe that one contractor laid carpet remnants on top of the 6 mil poly to try to reduce the number of holes and tears.

"Extreme Makeover – Crawl Space Edition"

I recommend a product called "CleanSpace®", which is made to perform to all the requirements aforementioned. CleanSpace is a 20 mil thick plastic liner, similar to a pool liner, that can be fitted in your crawl space to completely seal off your home from the earth.

CleanSpace has multiple layers of plastics with different characteristics of flexibility and puncture and tear resistance. Put together with two layers of polyester cord reinforcement, the material is incredibly durable, will last as long as the house, and will stay where you install it. To make things even better, CleanSpace is bright white, which dramatically transforms your crawl space from the nasty pit it was, to one you wouldn't hesitate to slide around in your socks in.

As an added benefit, CleanSpace has an antimicrobial additive manufactured into the material which prevents mold growth on the liner. This additive is odorless and safe, and is used in many plastic household and automotive products.

To satisfy the criteria for our crawl space walls – stopping water vapor and allowing for drainage to the sump – we install CleanSpace, fastening it to the upper part of the walls. We stay 3" down from the top of the walls so that termites cannot get to the framing without their mud tunnels being seen. The

Make Your Crawl Space a Clean Space. *At 20 mils thick, with polyester cord reinforcement inside, the CleanSpace crawl space liner is heavy and durable enough to line a crawl space.*

The CleanSpace Crawl Space Encapsulation System satisfies all of the repair criteria while dramatically transforming the space into healthy, useable space.

Crawl spaces with Existing Concrete Floors

6

Crawl spaces with concrete floors can be treated in the exact same manner – install a sump at the lowest spot and install a CleanSpace liner. One adaptation we can make is to lay down dimpled polyethylene drainage matting on the floor before installing the CleanSpace liner. This creates an air space for water to flow to the sump on top of the concrete floor.

We have done many of these jobs, which illustrates that pouring a concrete floor in a crawl space is not the answer to the problem.

CleanSpace liner is attached to the walls with fasteners along the top edge, which are permanently driven into holes drilled into the walls. With the criss-cross layers of polyester cord reinforcements within the CleanSpace liner, you cannot pull it off of the walls or tear the CleanSpace around the fasteners if you tried.

Satisfying our requirements that we need to allow drainage from the floor to the sump, and we must stop water vapor from permeating up from the floor is easy with this method. By laying the CleanSpace liner over the floor of the crawl space, water can seep or even flow under it to the sump, especially via any drainage channels you may have created before you installed it.

This crawl space has no more humidity than the space upstairs.

The liner is sealed around obstructions and at seams by a variety of methods, including special tapes and sealants. The top edge around the walls is sealed with urethane caulk. If the CleanSpace liner is on a sloped dirt floor, the liner can be staked to the floor so it doesn't move or pull downward when you crawl on it.

Another benefit of this method and material is that you can use your crawl space for storage after installation – something homeowners could never consider in a dirt crawl space.

CleanSpace is manufactured specifically for this purpose. As such it has an anti-microbial ingredient right in the plastic called "UltraFresh," which prevents mold and bacteria growth. It is used in other products such as plastic automotive air ducts to prevent mold.

A dimpled polyethylene membrane under the CleanSpace liner allows water to flow to a sump in a crawl space that already has a concrete floor.

! Provide for Plumbing Leaks in Your Crawl Space

Important

A plumbing leak in a dirt crawl space, will leak into the dirt forever (because you'll never notice it), keeping the dirt wet and the humidity up. When a CleanSpace system is installed, a plumbing leak can fill up your crawl space like a swimming pool. The sump systems described in Chapter 5, SuperSump and TripleSafe, have airtight lids with airtight floor drains that drain water from the top of the CleanSpace liner in the event of a plumbing leak in your crawl space.

If you don't have groundwater leakage you won't need a sump system in your crawl space with your CleanSpace system. However, you still need to provide for plumbing leaks. You can do this with a SmartDrain.

A SmartDrain is a drywell-type unit that gets installed in your crawl space along with the CleanSpace liner. It features an alarm and an airtight floor drain in its lid. In the event of a plumbing leak, the alarm sounds alerting you to the leak, and the water drains away into the soil under the CleanSpace until you get the leak fixed.

Side Note

Radon Gas

Radon is a naturally occurring radioactive gas that comes from radium deposits in the earth's crust. If present in the soil under your home, it can get sucked into your house via the basement or crawl space.

Don't panic. It's fairly common and easy to get rid of.

CleanSpace is a passive radon reduction system and method all by itself. If an "active" system needs to be installed, a fan can draw air from below the CleanSpace and exhaust it outside above the highest eave. In this case, CleanSpace represents the majority of the work and expense to get rid of the radon (if you have it), so it shouldn't cost much to add a fan and exhaust pipe.

Chapter 7

Step Three:
Seal Out 'EVIL' Outside Air

Now that you don't have any moisture from the earth, you don't need vents, which only made the moisture problem worse anyway, and drained you of energy dollars every month. So let's seal them up!

Special Crawl Space vent covers from Basement Systems are designed to do the trick. They are plastic so they won't rust or rot, and gasketed for an airtight seal using fasteners drilled into the wall.

BEFORE **AFTER**

Seal it. *The CleanSpace vent covers seal the air out, insulate, and improve the appearance.*

Important to Save Energy

This will make a **huge** improvement in your crawl space!

Important to Save Energy

Your Crawl Space Access Door Should Seal Tight

Insider Information

Important to Save Energy

Seal All Air Leaks to the Outside

Many crawl spaces have an access door to the outside. Most often it is made of plywood, and because it's down by the ground it rots easily. These rotted warped doors usually seal poorly and look like heck. The answer is an all-plastic door – that won't rot, warp, or need paint, and bugs won't eat it. Perfect.

Knobs screw into anchors in the wall to draw the door tight against weather-stripping to seal off outside air.

Before. *A rotting, loose-fitting, warped plywood door lets in lots of air.*

After. *A snug-fitting, all-plastic door stops air and moisture from entering.*

Once the liner is installed and the vents and air openings to the outside are closed, your crawl space will begin to dry out. There is just one step left, dehumidification...

When a CleanSpace system is installed, you want to seal vents to keep out evil unconditioned outside air. But vents aren't the only way outside air can get into your crawl space. Spaces under the sill plate and around pipes and wires to the outside, poorly fitting or rotted hatch doors, and other odd openings are all paths that need to be sealed to get the best results.

One area that was previously ignored is the open cavities in the top of block walls. Block walls are most common in dirt crawl spaces. Outside air goes right through porous block walls and up out of the top of the wall into the inside of the crawl space. To seal the top of the block walls, a product called "CleanSpace Wall Cap" works great. It's an "L"-shaped molding that slips right on top of the block wall covering the space the sill plate does not. The clear plastic allows for termite inspections without removing it.

Important to Save Energy

Keep Outside Air Out

Once the vents are sealed, then all other sources of outside air leakage into the crawl space need to be sealed. You may have a space between the sill plate and the top of the foundation that needs to be caulked. You may have openings around wires and pipes to the outside. You may have spaces or holes open to the garage, where unconditioned outside air is entering the crawl space. All these openings need to be sealed with caulk, flashing, spray foam, wood caulked in, or whatever material necessary.

Didn't Have a Chance. *Running a dehumidifier in a vented and/or dirt crawl space is pointless. You can never dehumidify a space that has exposed earth, or outside air leaking into it, or one that keeps leeaking water.*

Stop the EVIL Outside Air. *Seal all openings where outside air can get into your crawl space, such as along the sill plate, and around pipes and wires to the outside.*

You are on your way to a dry, energy-efficient crawl space – and a home that is less expensive, more comfortable, and healthier to live in!

Clear Skies Ahead

Chapter 8

Step Four:
Keep Your Crawl Space Air Dry

A dehumidification system is the "cherry on top" of your crawl space solution.

This **BIG** is a IDEA!

Mastering Humidity – The Anti-Mold

Even though we have sealed off the earth and sealed air leaks to the outside, we will still have some air infiltration. Air is a very small thing and our crawl space sucks air in through the tiniest of spaces. And since our crawl space is cool relative to incoming summer air, we are raising its relative humidity once it enters. There are a few solutions – the best one being dehumidification. Correction. I should say efficient and effective dehumidification.

Not so easy to do unless you have the right equipment. It just so happens that we do...

In order to eliminate condensation you need to either heat the air (ridiculous in summer), or take water out of it (easy to do). Correction. I should say take water out of it *efficiently and effectively* (not so easy unless you have the right equipment to do it with).

Not Just Any Dehumidifier

A dehumidifier is the plain answer. But not just any dehumidifier. I have been dealing with this issue intensely for nearly 20 years. The only machine that will get you the results you need is one called a SaniDry Basement Air System. And it's awesome.

The SaniDry is a high-capacity, high-efficiency dehumidification system, with air filtration, in a single unit. The SaniDry takes up to 100 pints of water per day out of your crawl space air, while using the same energy as a "40 pint" dehumidifier. And it filters particles out of the air to less than an incredible two microns in size – which is smaller than any mold spore or dust mite dropping.

Not Just on Concrete. *Condensation can form on cold water pipes and ducts too.*

You'll *really* Love This!

The SaniDry Air System wrings your air dry, and its powerful blower moves that dry air out into and around your crawl space. This dry air then dries your building materials and contents, which makes the damp smell and damp feeling go away! What a huge difference a SaniDry can make in "condensation season." People really love their dry crawl spaces after having a SaniDry installed.

◀

Cacti Only. *The SaniDry Air System will dry any basement or crawl space – no matter how damp – and keep them that way! (upright model shown in a basement)*

You'll also never have to empty any buckets on your SaniDry system because it automatically drains into your sump system (there are other alternatives if you don't have a sump system).

Having a groundwater-free basement is one thing. Adding a SaniDry is like putting the cherry on top of your dry crawl space program. It makes it complete.

8

How does it perform so incredibly well with the same amount of energy that less-effective 20-pound-weakling dehumidifiers use?

1. The SaniDry blows air over a huge cold coil. It looks like a truck radiator instead of the little squirrelly spiral coil of dinky dehumidifiers.

2. The SaniDry runs the exiting dry cold air through a special heat-exchange core that pre-cools the incoming wet air and recaptures energy.

3. The SaniDry's powerful 200 cfm blower not only grabs more air in to dry faster, but moves the dry air out around your crawl space to dry all the nooks and crannies of your floor system above.

There are other component reasons SaniDry wins the dehumidifier battle, but these are the main ones.

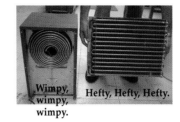

Wimpy, wimpy, wimpy. Hefty, Hefty, Hefty.

Powerful blower. *200 cfm blower really moves dehumidified air around to dry the entire space.*

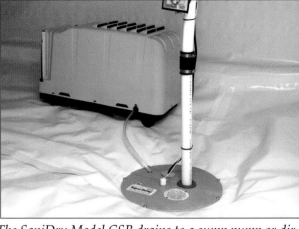

The SaniDry Model CSB drains to a sump pump or directly outside so you never have to empty a bucket again.

A Colorado crawl space is fitted with a CleanSpace crawl space encapsulation system. A duct carries dried air from a SaniDry Air System located upstairs. ▼

To further prove its mettle, SaniDry is Energy Star rated – a rare achievement for a dehumidification system. Another big benefit of the SaniDry system is that it doesn't have to be located in the space it's drying. In very short crawl spaces you can locate the SaniDry in a utility room upstairs and duct the wet air in and dry air out to the crawl space.

With no water leaks and dry air, materials stay dry and you can finish your basement or use it for storage.
No smell, no mold, no property damage.

Did I mention I love the SaniDry system? And you will too.

Why Household Dehumidifiers Just Don't Do the Job

1. They are too small.

2. The cold coil (the actual thing that takes the water out of the air) is too small.

3. The fan is too small (it has to be so it doesn't blow the air past the dinky coil too fast, otherwise it wouldn't take <u>any</u> water out!)

4. The fan doesn't circulate the dry air around your crawl space – because it's too small.

5. They usually aren't drained automatically, so the bucket fills up and they shut off.

6. They are rated (25 pints, 30 pints, 40 pints, etc.) per day *at 80 degrees* air temperature. Warm air holds a lot more moisture than cold air. Put them in a 68 degree basement and their effectiveness goes way down below this number.

There is simply no comparison between a SaniDry Air System and any dehumidifier you've ever seen.
I am usually a bit conservative and always realistic about what a product can do. The SaniDry Air System is one product where I let all the performance promises hang out.

Apples & Oranges

CAUTION

Open Sump Hole?

Having an open sump hole and running a dehumidifier is like trying to fill a bucket with a hole in it. As you dry the air, more water evaporates into it via the open sump hole with a pool of water sitting in it all year. In other words you have a dehumidifier and a humidifier.

8

Dehumidifiers Should Drain Automatically

Quick –

How many hours in a week?
168.

How long would it take a cheapo dehumidifier's bucket to fill up and shut off?
Maybe 12.

If you empty it once a week, what percentage of the time is it actually running? If you're not a mathlete, the answer is **7% of the time**. Meaning it's <u>off</u> for 93% of the time.

Who wants to have "Empty dehumidifier bucket" on their daily chore sheet? The answer is to hook it up with a hose to **automatically drain the water away** – and you never have to empty it.

What Makes a Crawl Space Smell Like One?

Answer = Mold.

Mold can grow in a "waterproofed crawl space."

Mold needs organic material to grow (which you have), and high relative humidity – over 60 to 70%. It doesn't have to be wet for mold to grow, just humid. In fact, mold won't grow underwater.

A SaniDry Air System ensures that the relative humidity stays below 55% all year long so mold doesn't have a chance. The SaniDry can keep your Relative Humidity well below 55%, but there is no additional benefit to keeping it that low.

The SaniDry (Model CS shown) automatically drains into a SuperSump.

◀  ▶

Save Money
Dry Air is Easier to Cool!

Damp indoor air costs more money to cool. Sure, a SaniDry costs a bit in electricity to run, but lower cooling costs in part offset this electric cost. This is because your central air system has to remove the moisture from the air in order to cool it, and that takes energy. Air conditioning systems are inefficient at dehumidifying.

If you dry the air in your crawl space, that air rises into the rest of the house, making the whole house drier.

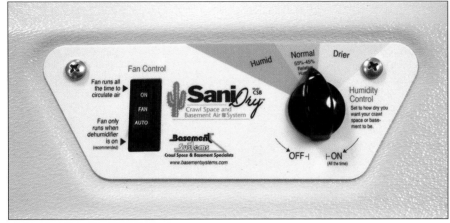

Important to Save Energy

Apples & Oranges

SaniDry – Energy Test Winner!

We tested four dehumidifiers to find out the cost per pint of water removed from the air. The worst performer was a standard household unit available under any number of recognizable brand names. It came out at more than 11 cents per pint removed. A higher priced unit, but one without the features of the SaniDry, costs about 10 cents per pint of water removed. The big winner was the SaniDry, which costs only 3.3 cents per pint of water removed! What a bargain!

Dust Mites – #1 Indoor Allergen

The number one thing that people with asthma and allergies react to indoors is dust mite droppings. These parasites live in your furniture, bedding, and carpeting, and feed off dead skin flakes. Their droppings are so small that they become airborne, are breathed in, and thus can irritate humans. Dust mites need relative humidity above 50% to live, as they absorb water out of the air rather than drinking it. Therefore, dry the air and dust mites die.

We have heard of a story of a doctor in West Virginia prescribing a SaniDry unit on his prescription pad! Now there's an enlightened doctor!

For more information go to www.housedustmite.org

8

8

The SaniDry is a very effective and energy efficient dehumidifier, and can be located in the crawl space.

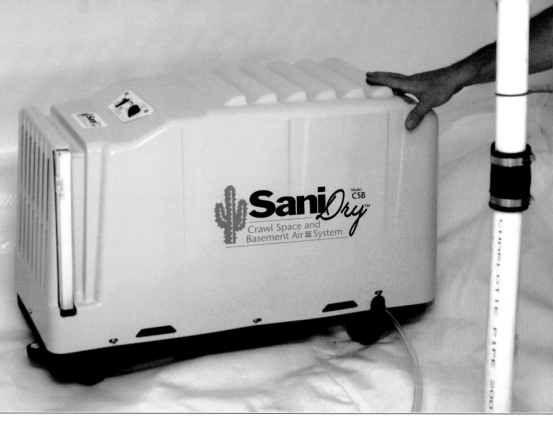

O ur SaniDry CSB model is configured for crawl spaces with low ceiling height. Your dealer will pick the right model for you – you really can't go wrong.

Break out the Chapstick. SaniDry really dries out your crawl space.

SaniDry CSB's low profile, air filtration, and heavy-duty drying make this the perfect crawl space dehumidifier.

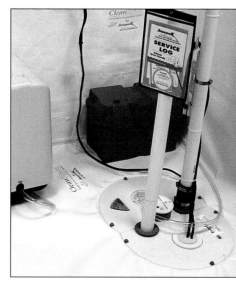

Floor Insulation – Now You Need It, Now You Don't

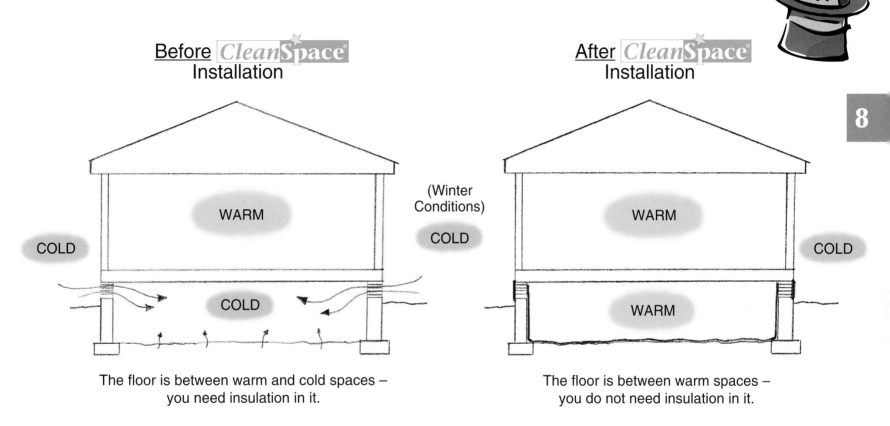

Before *Clean*Space®
Installation

After *Clean*Space®
Installation

(Winter Conditions)

WARM

COLD

COLD

COLD

WARM

COLD

COLD

WARM

The floor is between warm and cold spaces –
you need insulation in it.

The floor is between warm spaces –
you do not need insulation in it.

A fter a CleanSpace installation, you do not need insulation in the floor. So if it's moldy or in bad shape otherwise, you can remove it and not worry about replacing it. By closing vents, sealing other air leaks, and installing CleanSpace, you are making a world of difference in your home's energy efficiency. If you want to take a next incremental step, a radiant barrier could be installed on the walls, or the walls can be insulated with foam boards, either under or over the CleanSpace on the walls.

Dryer Vents – as Evil as Air Comes

8

Never vent a dryer into a crawl space. All that water from your skivvys will cause a big moisture problem in your crawl space – no matter what season it is. Duct dryer vents outside.

A dryer vent only adds to the moisture load in your crawl space.

Duct Leakage
First Your Enemy, Now Your Friend

(Skip if you have hot water heat)

As we said, duct leakage only serves to distribute damp, moldy air throughout the house from a vented dirt crawl space, as well as distributing some of your energy dollars out the window (or rather, out the <u>vents</u>).

But after the vents to the outside are sealed and a CleanSpace system is installed, duct leakage which could be 300 cubic feet of air per minute, is your friend.

Why? Because it distributes conditioned (heated, cooled, dried) air from your HVAC system into and out of your crawl space. This dries your crawl space. And since there is no way for the air to get out of the crawl space to the exterior, it only serves to help the upstairs environment. For example, heat leaking out of a supply duct will rise and warm and dry the floors above and make the first floor cheaper to heat with warm floors instead of the cold floors you had before.

And duct leakage is an accidental way to get combustion air into a crawl space too. Just make sure that there are no big holes in the <u>return</u> ducts.

"Conditioning" Your Crawl Space

We described a lot about using a super-duper unit called a SaniDry or SaniDry CSB Air System.

Remember it's not just the crawl space you are dehumidifying. Because air rises from the bottom to top of your home, the air that now rises will dry your house instead of wetting it.

Another way to dry the air in your crawl space is to "condition" it. This means you use the Heating and Air Conditioning System to heat, cool, and dry the crawl space. Because your crawl space is low it doesn't really tax your system very much at all. In fact, because warm air rises to heat the floors above, it costs almost nothing as long as you have a complete CleanSpace system installed and seal the vents and other air openings to the outside.

One way to condition a crawl space is to constantly blow a small amount of air from upstairs into the crawl space. You can do this with a "Crawl-O-Sphere air machine." Depending on the size of your crawl space, this system draws from between 15 and 80 cubic feet of air per minute from the upstairs and blows it into your crawl space.

The air from upstairs is dry in the summer (if you have central air conditioning) and warm and dry in the winter, and for little cost, will dry your crawl space pretty well. It is not as effective as a SaniDry, but the Crawl-O-Sphere machine is a lower-cost alternative.

Combustion Appliances

If you have a furnace or water heater in your crawl space that requires air to burn for combustion of gas or oil, you may need to allow air to enter the crawl space for that purpose. This air, once used to burn fuel, goes up the chimney. The idea is if you create a vacuum in your crawl space because you sealed it up so tight, then you will not have a draft to take exhaust gases up the chimney from your furnace or water heater.

We are talking about appliances that are "atmospherically vented", meaning they take in air for combustion from around their metal enclosures from the room they are in. Your water heater and HVAC unit are most likely atmospherically vented.

When I think about the thousands of basements I have been in, even small ones, which almost always have combustion appliances in them, I can probably count on one hand the times I have seen fresh combustion air for them. They draw in air from inside the building to burn and exhaust up the chimney. There is enough air leakage in a basement, even without vents, that adequate combustion air is not a problem.

"Normal air infiltration" in a building is considered adequate by the building code for combustion air supply. However, a crawl space is smaller than a basement, and you are sealing it up tight as part of your strategy to stop moisture. If there are combustion appliances located in the crawl space, there has to be a way for them to get air to maintain proper draft all of the time.

YOU MUST NOT DEPRESSURIZE A SPACE WHERE COMBUSTION APPLIANCES ARE LOCATED.

One easy way to provide combustion air is to install two vents in the crawl space ceiling to the first floor. This way air can be drawn down into the crawl space if the combustion appliances need it. It's better than the alternative, which is to leave a vent to the outside open where "evil" unconditioned (hot, cold, wet) outside air can enter. The International Residential Code 2000 allows for the installation of vents to adjoining indoor spaces for combustion air.

A combustion air supply unit is a good option. One unit called the "Inforcer™" is a fan unit wired to your burner circuit. When the burner turns on, the fan blows in make-up air, and when the burner is off, a damper closes to prevent outdoor air entry. For more information go to www.tjernlund.com.

For new homes, or when replacing your water heater or HVAC unit, you should use "direct vent" appliances, instead of "atmospherically vented" ones. Direct vent appliances have a place where you attach a dedicated combustion air supply duct to the outside. This satisfies the whole combustion air supply issue, without having to worry about where or how to vent in combustion air.

It is important to have a (CO) carbon monoxide alarm if you have combustion appliances or attached garages.

There are performance protocols available from Advanced Energy (www.advancedenergy.org) to confirm the safe performance of combustion appliances following building changes. You can have a test done to ensure combustion air is not a problem.

8

8

Save 15% – 20% on Energy Costs

An independent study revealed that homeowners who properly fix their vented dirt crawl space can save 15% - 20% on their heating and air conditioning costs!

Fixing Your Crawl Space Pays for itself!

**You'll Love
This!**

On one hand, one could argue that the net costs to fix a crawl space is zero, since it saves money each month in energy costs, and you avoid costly rot and mold repairs. In fact you could say it doesn't cost, it pays, since you will eventually save more than it costs.

Nevertheless, there is an investment up front to have the work done, and the savings accrues over the years. For a 1500 square foot crawl space you can expect to pay about $9,000 for a solution involving concrete, and about $5,300 and up for one using a liner like CleanSpace. There are variables to consider. The size of your crawl space, the height of your crawl space, how much drainage work you may or may not need, the sump, the battery back-up pump, and dehumidification are all things that will change what you can expect to pay. A complete system in a large home could cost much more than that.

One thing is for sure. You can't justify what you paid for your home and then say it's okay to let the conditions in your crawl space fester and threaten your investment in your home.

CleanSpace is one of those things that you are going to pay for whether you get it or not. This makes it a no-brainer to get it!

Fixing your crawl space properly is probably the smartest and most financially rewarding home repair you'll ever make.

Crawl Space No – No's

- Don't put a vapor barrier or rigid insulation board on the ceiling of your crawl space (unless your home is on stilts).

- Don't close vents without sealing the earth.

- Don't seal the earth without closing the vents.

- Never use a fan to blow outside air into your crawl space.

- Never use a fan to blow air out of your crawl space.

- Don't install a liner or concrete without removing organic material such as wood, cardboard, insulation, etc., from the dirt floor first.

- Don't depressurize a space that has combustion appliances (more than one pascal).

- Don't run your dryer vent into your crawl space.

- Don't ignore the problem.

A vapor barrier on the bottom of floor joists traps water above it to rot joists.

8

(Photo- Advanced Energy) Power fans like this can make your mold, moisture, rot and energy problems worse – fast!

Rigid insulation board on the crawl space ceiling creates a moisture pocket against the floor joists.

Chapter 9

Lies the Building Code Told Me...

The building code allows dirt crawl spaces that are vented. In fact, they require them to be vented. Recently in the 2000 International Residential Code, they have added exceptions to the venting provision (which don't make complete sense to me).

One exception says "where warranted by climactic conditions, ventilation openings to the outdoors are not required if ventilation openings to the interior are provided". So you can have a dirt crawl space and vent it to the inside of your home? And what climactic conditions are they talking about anyway?

At least these exceptions give us a hint that some people who write the code know that something isn't right.

Don't get me wrong; homes in the U.S. today are safer than those in many other countries because of our building code. That's great. The building code protects us. But on the crawl space issue, the code has been so wrong for so many years. Twenty years ago we could chalk it up to ignorance. But now we know what the problem is.

How long can it be before someone points to the building code and says, "this rotted my house", or "this is responsible for the mold in my house"?

There is a document from the Department of Energy that says vented dirt crawl spaces are wrong, and to close the vents. It goes on to say that they recognize that this is against the building code, so you might have to pull some creative explanation to get by the local inspector. Try calling it a "short basement", the Feds say, so the locals will allow it. It's really ridiculous.

So what should the code writers do? In my opinion, they should act now and change the code to disallow exposed earth under a house, and forbid venting crawl spaces. They should admit their error in light of new research, and get it over with. It's inevitable, so why wait any longer?

In some states, Arkansas for one, a division of the Department of Agriculture is somehow ordained with the job of moisture control in crawl spaces. Why? As near as I can tell, pest control operators such as termite contractors go into crawl spaces all the time, and do "moisture control work" under homes. Since they use pesticides, which are regulated by the Dept. of Agriculture, then the same department got the "regulation of moisture control". These boards insist on ventilation. And if there is mold or rot, their solution is to add more vents. It has never worked. These boards must look at the evidence and compare it against evidence of their own that supports ventilation (of which there is none), and change their codes accordingly. A code is not evidence that it works, no matter how old the code is!

One thing we have heard in the field is that some termite contractors won't warrant the house against termites if there is a liner in the crawl space. They say that they can't see the termites if they are there. This is just plain resistance to change and fear of what they don't understand. However many are changing their mind on this issue.

A dry house is less likely to get eaten by termites. We leave a 3" strip of foundation wall exposed at the top so they can inspect for termites anyway. Besides, what would they do if the crawl space had a concrete floor in it? What would they do if it were a basement? How about a finished basement where you can't see the floor or walls? Are we to say that you cannot finish your basement because the termite guy can't see the walls and floor, and if you can't get your termite warranty your bank won't let you close on the mortgage, so you can't buy the house or refinance? This is ridiculous.

9

What termite contractors have to fear is that all of their customers with moldy crawl spaces will come back to them and say that on their recommendation they added vents that caused their house to rot. You can rightly chalk it up to old codes and ignorance until now. Now the new research is out and it's time for a change.

One of our dealers in South Carolina installed a CleanSpace system and sealed the vents in a home, which was then inspected by a home inspector before the house was sold. The home inspector told the buyer that the crawl space was illegally sealed up, and that it would surely rot unless it was put back the way it was. He really went on about how bad it was.

So our dealer hired Craig DeWitt PhD, an engineer who specializes in moisture and energy issues, to come in and do an assessment. Craig measured the Relative Humidity and wood moisture content and found them to be far less (better) than the average conditions seen in vented dirt crawl spaces in the area. He issued a report saying, "the crawl space in its current configuration, is providing a durable, high-performance foundation system ... that will outperform a vented crawl space."

In all fairness to industry professionals, they are just going by what they've always done. We all learn things from other people, and they have accepted the "old way" without doing any research, and without making the observation that it is not working. Some termite contractors, code officials, and building inspectors are on the leading edge of this issue, although they are the minority as of this writing. The rest need to be enlightened. The good news is that it's simple, and it doesn't hurt.

All truth goes through 3 stages –

First it is ridiculed,
Then it is violently opposed,
Then it's accepted as self-evident.

-Schopenhauer

"This house was built according to Building Code."

9

CLOSE
CLOSED

Chapter 10

Crawl Space Repair Projects
Heaven and Hell

Take care of the leakage/drainage problem, isolate the house from the earth, and close all outside air leaks, and you'll save money each month, and make your house a healthier, more comfortable place to live.

Before

After

Hell

Heaven

Before

After

Before

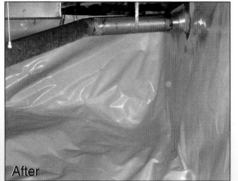
After

Before

After

All these homeowners were extremely happy that they took action. Now they are experiencing energy savings every month! These are all photos of the CleanSpace® Crawl Space Encapsulation™ System.

CleanSpace ® *Heaven*

You'll Love This!

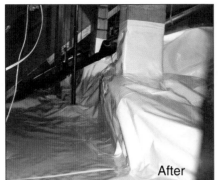

After

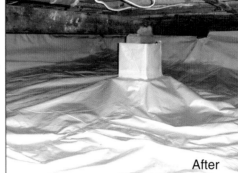

After

These homes will last decades longer with the CleanSpace System.

After

After

More CleanSpace Heaven

After

After

After

After

10

Before

After

10

Chapter 11

The Perfect Crawl Space Under Your Feet
If Money's No Object, Then Do This

Money is an object!

Okay, it is. But only if you expected to pay cash for this repair. Most people don't pay cash for an automobile – they finance it. There are all kinds of options to get your crawl space fixed right – a home equity loan, credit cards, or a home improvement loan with which your dealer can help you.

If a house is worth owning for what you paid for it, with a wet, damp, moldy lower level that causes property damage, rot, poor health, frustration, and despair, then it is worth owning with a dry, healthy space for what you paid for it plus $10,000. Make sense?

You'll Love This!

Important to Save Energy

CleanSpace, Crawl Space Encapsulation System with a TripleSafe Sump System and SaniDry Crawl Space Air System.

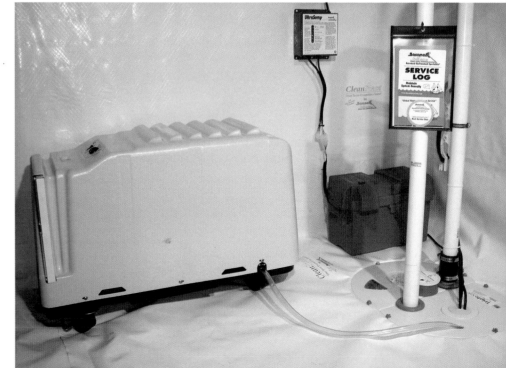

You'll Love This!

The Perfect Solution

1. CleanSpace drainage matting on the floor with a CleanSpace encapsulation system with anti-microbial ingredient.....................................see chapter 6

2. A TripleSafe Sump Pump System with IceGuard System
(for crawl spaces with groundwater leakage, are graded to sump location, or SmartDrain for crawl spaces with no ground water leakage)..........................see chapter 8

3. SaniDry Air System ....see chapter 8

4. CleanSpace Vent Covers..see chapter 3

5. An EverLast Crawl Space Door
(if your door is leaky. Wall Cap if you have open topped block walls.
All other outside air leaks sealed) .... see chapter 7

**Estimated price for a 1500 square foot crawl space
and with TripleSafe Sump System - $9,800**

The price will vary widely with how big the crawl space is, the amount of drainage work, vents, doors, sump equipment, etc. Consult your local basement Systems dealer or CleanSpace installer for a written estimate and exact price in your home.

Buyers Expect a Dry Crawl Space

This is a BIG IDEA!

Who wants to buy a home with a damp, moldy crawl space? Nobody! It's difficult enough to find a buyer who wants your house, and heart-breaking when they walk away after looking at the crawl space.

These days in most states there are disclosure forms which ask the seller a whole range of questions about their knowledge of defects with the property. One of the questions asks if you ever had any mold in the home. In addition, most buyers hire home inspectors these days to inspect the property for defects. Home inspectors have a keen eye for moisture and mold problems because that's what they are hired for.

There is simply no hiding your crawl space problem when you sell your home. And if you do disclose your crawl space problem, either nobody will buy, or they will make a low offer. In fact, buyers will discount the price of a home by 10% or more because of a damp, moldy crawl space.

10% is a lot of money!

Because buyers view your home with a damp, moldy crawl space as a fixer-upper, they will pay you 10% less than otherwise – that's if they buy it at all. Using this example then –

If your home is worth-	The cost of not fixing your crawl space in property value _alone_ is-
$100,000	$10,000
$150,000	$15,000
$200,000	$20,000
$300,000	$30,000
$400,000	$40,000
$500,000	$50,000
$600,000	$60,000

You get the idea. And this does not take into account the cost of mold remediation, rot repairs, or higher energy bills each month while you live there!

The Moral of the Story
–Fixing your crawl space is a lot cheaper than not fixing your crawl space!

Remember, you are going to spend more if you <u>don't</u> fix it!

Now you know the very latest cutting-edge "Crawl Space Science." You are an educated consumer and know what to have done to your home and why. Your local Basement Systems dealer can help you with the items discussed in this book because we know all of this stuff and live it everyday. Beware of those who try to imitate and those who say, "We can do what Basement Systems does too." Anyone can say that, but they can't do it. To find your local dealer, call 1-800-640-1500. Thank you!

We're There. The Basement Systems dealer network spans North America, the United Kingdom, and Ireland.

Ireland

United Kingdom

Basement Systems Patents

Basement Systems Inc. holds more than 23 patents and has others pending on ideas and products discussed in this book. We also have many trademarks.

Patent Notices

Obviously we do not want others violating our patents. However, we very much want to work with those who would like to fix their crawl spaces, and work with contractors who would like to get involved.

Please contact us at 1-800-768-6815 and ask for the CleanSpace department, or visit www.basementsystems.com. We welcome inquiries and will find a way to work with you.

These and all Basement Systems logos are registered trademarks of Basement Systems Inc.

CleanSpace
Crawl Space Encapsulation System
CleanSpace Vent Covers
SmartDrain
CleanSpace Wall Cap
EverLast Crawl Space Door
Crawl-O-Sphere Air System
SuperSump System
TripleSafe System
IceGuard System
WaterWatch Alarm System
CleanPump Stand

Acknowledgments

Some people may think that crawl spaces are unglamorous, uncelebrated, and unimportant. Unglamorous and uncelebrated, yes. Unimportant, no! When it's what you do everyday, and you can save homeowners billions of dollars every year, protecting assets and improving health for millions, it's very important. My vision is that we stop building these energy wasting nasty holes under our homes, and fix all 26 million of them out there.

I would like to acknowledge the following people and groups for their contributions.

My wife Wendy and my children Tanner, Chloe and Autumn.

Mike Delmolino and Lou Bemer at Basement Systems CleanSpace Department.

Joe Lstiburek, and his Building Science Corp. www.buildingscience.com.

Craig Dewitt at RLC Engineering, Clemson, SC. www.RLCengineering.com.

Fine Homebuilding Magazine, for publishing my article "Sealing Crawl Spaces" in their March, 2003 issue, Number 153. www.finehomebuilding.com.

Royce Lewis at Comfort Diagnostics in Little Rock Arkansas.

Chris Sullivan at Moisture Solutions in Conway, Arkansas.

Kevin Koval at Adirondack Basement Systems in Clifton Park, New York.

Rod Martin at Complete Basement Systems of Denver, Colorado, and Pete Karreman at Omni Basement Systems in Toronto, for photos.

Harold Shapiro, photographer, Branford, Connecticut.

Jeff Nelson, Chad Achenbach, Greg Smith, Sam Bullock, Jason Woods, Charlene Bieber, and many others at Connecticut Basement Systems, for photos.

The staff at my company, Basement Systems Inc, and our many dealers, who are helping to make the world a better place by fixing crawl spaces everyday. www.basementsystems.com.

Advanced Energy, for their research and charts, and photos. www.advancedenergy.org.

Dan Fitzgerald and Richard Fencil for their great editing.

Mike Delmolino—
"Captain CleanSpace"

About the Author

After five years as a carpenter and builder, Larry Janesky founded Basement Systems Inc. in 1987 to provide basement waterproofing services to existing homes. He soon learned that there was much room for improvement in the industry, and set out to make those improvements. He has since patented 23 products, with more pending and even more in various stages of design and development.

Larry is currently the president of the world's largest basement waterproofing and crawl space repair dealer network, Basement Systems Inc., that specializes in developing and providing products that result in dry below-ground environments. The company has won three business ethics awards, two consumer education awards, many quality and innovation awards, and was named one of the "20 Best Places to Work" in Connecticut. Larry and his company have fixed thousands of crawl spaces since 1987.

Larry has been invited to a number of industry conventions to discuss his research and solutions. Larry has trained more than 3000 people over the last 16 years on basement waterproofing and crawl space repair. His articles have been published in *Fine Homebuilding* magazine, *Permanent Buildings and Foundations* magazine, and other publications. He wrote the book on fixing wet basements entitled, "Dry Basement Science."

Larry enjoys his free time in rural Connecticut with his son Tanner, daughters Chloe and Autumn, and his lovely wife Wendy. There he also builds and rides on his motocross track and ATV trails.

You can read more about Basement Systems Inc., basement waterproofing, below-grade environments, and the CleanSpace® Crawl Space Encapsulation™ System, at www.basementsystems.com.